Bourbon Tasting Logbook

THIS BELONGS TO :	
PHONE :	
EMAIL :	
START DATE :	
LAST DATE :	

CONTENTS

PAGE	BOURBON NAME	PAGE	BOURBON NAME
4		29	
5		30	
6		31	
7		32	
8		33	
9		34	
10		35	
11		36	
12		37	
13		38	
14		39	
15		40	
16		41	
17		42	
18		43	
19		44	
20		45	
21		46	
22		47	
23		48	
24		49	
25		50	
26		51	
27		52	
28		53	

CONTENTS

PAGE	BOURBON NAME	PAGE	BOURBON NAME
54		79	
55		80	
56		81	
57		82	
58		83	
59		84	
60		85	
61		86	
62		87	
63		88	
64		89	
65		90	
66		91	
67		92	
68		93	
69		94	
70		95	
71		96	
72		97	
73		98	
74		99	
75		100	
76		101	
77		102	
78		103	

BOURBON NAME :		DATE TASTED :	
DISTILLERY :		TYPE / GRADE :	
COUNTRY ORIGIN :		AGE :	
SAMPLED :		PRICE :	
BOTTLE SIZE :		ALCOHOL :	

COLOR METER

- BLACK
- BARK BROWN
- MAHOGANY
- BRICK
- DARK AMBER
- AMBER
- GOLD
- STRAW
- CLEAR

FLAVOR WHEEL

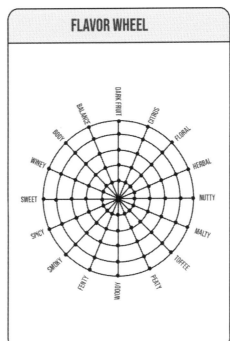

FLAVOR NOTES

FINAL RATING		ADDITIONAL NOTES
APPEARANCE :	☆☆☆☆☆	
TASTE :	☆☆☆☆☆	
MOUTHFEEL :	☆☆☆☆☆	
OVERALL RATING :	☆☆☆☆☆	

BOURBON NAME :		DATE TASTED :	
DISTILLERY :		TYPE / GRADE :	
COUNTRY ORIGIN :		AGE :	
SAMPLED :		PRICE :	
BOTTLE SIZE :		ALCOHOL :	

COLOR METER

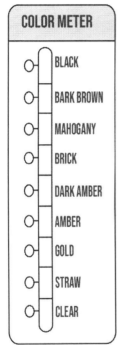

- BLACK
- BARK BROWN
- MAHOGANY
- BRICK
- DARK AMBER
- AMBER
- GOLD
- STRAW
- CLEAR

FLAVOR WHEEL

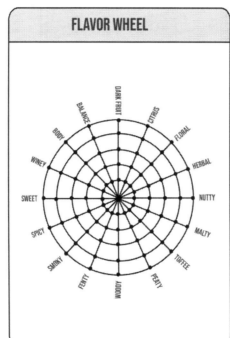

FLAVOR NOTES

FINAL RATING		ADDITIONAL NOTES
APPEARANCE :	☆☆☆☆☆	
TASTE :	☆☆☆☆☆	
MOUTHFEEL :	☆☆☆☆☆	
OVERALL RATING :	☆☆☆☆☆	

🍾 BOURBON NAME :		📅 DATE TASTED :	
🏭 DISTILLERY :		🥃 TYPE / GRADE :	
🌍 COUNTRY ORIGIN :		👥 AGE :	
🥃 SAMPLED :		🏷️ PRICE :	
🍾 BOTTLE SIZE :		🧪 ALCOHOL :	

COLOR METER

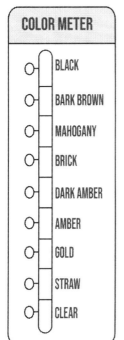

- BLACK
- BARK BROWN
- MAHOGANY
- BRICK
- DARK AMBER
- AMBER
- GOLD
- STRAW
- CLEAR

FLAVOR WHEEL

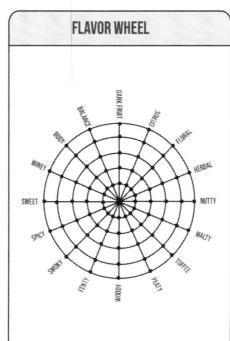

FLAVOR NOTES

FINAL RATING		ADDITIONAL NOTES
🏭 APPEARANCE :	☆☆☆☆☆	
👅 TASTE :	☆☆☆☆☆	
👄 MOUTHFEEL :	☆☆☆☆☆	
🏆 OVERALL RATING :	☆☆☆☆☆	

BOURBON NAME :		DATE TASTED :	
DISTILLERY :		TYPE / GRADE :	
COUNTRY ORIGIN :		AGE :	
SAMPLED :		PRICE :	
BOTTLE SIZE :		ALCOHOL :	

COLOR METER

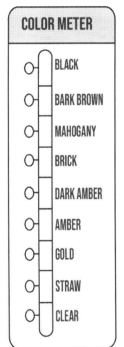

- BLACK
- BARK BROWN
- MAHOGANY
- BRICK
- DARK AMBER
- AMBER
- GOLD
- STRAW
- CLEAR

FLAVOR WHEEL

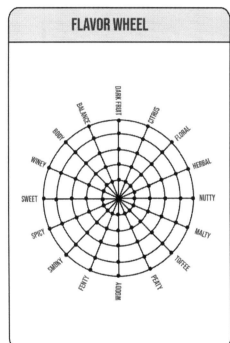

FLAVOR NOTES

FINAL RATING | ADDITIONAL NOTES

APPEARANCE :	☆☆☆☆☆	
TASTE :	☆☆☆☆☆	
MOUTHFEEL :	☆☆☆☆☆	
OVERALL RATING :	☆☆☆☆☆	

🏛️ BOURBON NAME :		📅 DATE TASTED :	
🏭 DISTILLERY :		🏷️ TYPE / GRADE :	
🌍 COUNTRY ORIGIN :		👥 AGE :	
🥃 SAMPLED :		🏷️ PRICE :	
🍾 BOTTLE SIZE :		🧾 ALCOHOL :	

COLOR METER

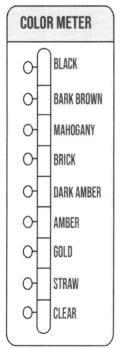

- BLACK
- BARK BROWN
- MAHOGANY
- BRICK
- DARK AMBER
- AMBER
- GOLD
- STRAW
- CLEAR

FLAVOR WHEEL

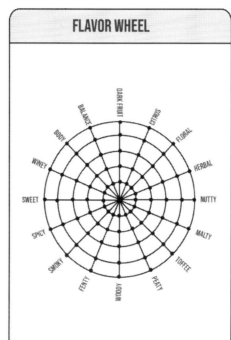

FLAVOR NOTES

FINAL RATING		ADDITIONAL NOTES
🏛️ APPEARANCE :	☆☆☆☆☆	
👃 TASTE :	☆☆☆☆☆	
👄 MOUTHFEEL :	☆☆☆☆☆	
🏆 OVERALL RATING :	☆☆☆☆☆	

BOURBON NAME :		DATE TASTED :	
DISTILLERY :		TYPE / GRADE :	
COUNTRY ORIGIN :		AGE :	
SAMPLED :		PRICE :	
BOTTLE SIZE :		ALCOHOL :	

COLOR METER

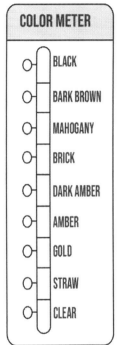

- BLACK
- BARK BROWN
- MAHOGANY
- BRICK
- DARK AMBER
- AMBER
- GOLD
- STRAW
- CLEAR

FLAVOR WHEEL

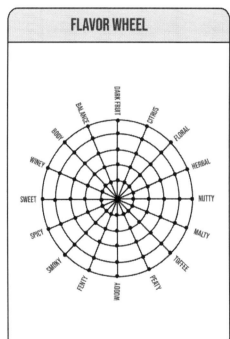

FLAVOR NOTES

FINAL RATING

		ADDITIONAL NOTES
APPEARANCE :	☆☆☆☆☆	
TASTE :	☆☆☆☆☆	
MOUTHFEEL :	☆☆☆☆☆	
OVERALL RATING :	☆☆☆☆☆	

BOURBON NAME :		DATE TASTED :	
DISTILLERY :		TYPE / GRADE :	
COUNTRY ORIGIN :		AGE :	
SAMPLED :		PRICE :	
BOTTLE SIZE :		ALCOHOL :	

COLOR METER

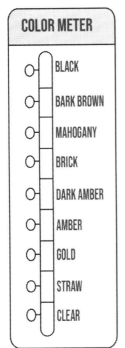

- BLACK
- BARK BROWN
- MAHOGANY
- BRICK
- DARK AMBER
- AMBER
- GOLD
- STRAW
- CLEAR

FLAVOR WHEEL

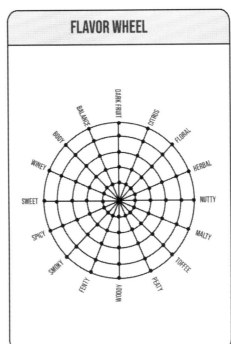

BALANCE · DARK FRUIT · CITRUS · FLORAL · HERBAL · NUTTY · MALTY · TOFFEE · PEATY · WOODY · PEATY · SMOKY · SPICY · SWEET · WINEY · BODY

FLAVOR NOTES

FINAL RATING		ADDITIONAL NOTES
APPEARANCE :	☆☆☆☆☆	
TASTE :	☆☆☆☆☆	
MOUTHFEEL :	☆☆☆☆☆	
OVERALL RATING :	☆☆☆☆☆	

BOURBON NAME :		**DATE TASTED :**	
DISTILLERY :		**TYPE / GRADE :**	
COUNTRY ORIGIN :		**AGE :**	
SAMPLED :		**PRICE :**	
BOTTLE SIZE :		**ALCOHOL :**	

COLOR METER

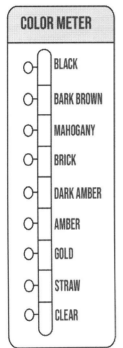

FLAVOR WHEEL

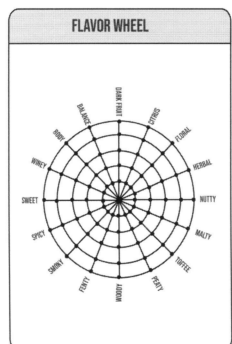

FLAVOR NOTES

FINAL RATING		ADDITIONAL NOTES
APPEARANCE :	☆☆☆☆☆	
TASTE :	☆☆☆☆☆	
MOUTHFEEL :	☆☆☆☆☆	
OVERALL RATING :	☆☆☆☆☆	

BOURBON NAME :		**DATE TASTED :**	
DISTILLERY :		**TYPE / GRADE :**	
COUNTRY ORIGIN :		**AGE :**	
SAMPLED :		**PRICE :**	
BOTTLE SIZE :		**ALCOHOL :**	

COLOR METER

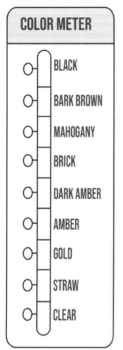

- BLACK
- BARK BROWN
- MAHOGANY
- BRICK
- DARK AMBER
- AMBER
- GOLD
- STRAW
- CLEAR

FLAVOR WHEEL

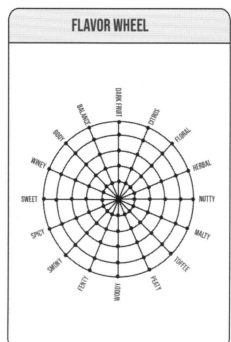

FLAVOR NOTES

FINAL RATING		ADDITIONAL NOTES
APPEARANCE :	☆☆☆☆☆	
TASTE :	☆☆☆☆☆	
MOUTHFEEL :	☆☆☆☆☆	
OVERALL RATING :	☆☆☆☆☆	

BOURBON NAME :		DATE TASTED :	
DISTILLERY :		TYPE / GRADE :	
COUNTRY ORIGIN :		AGE :	
SAMPLED :		PRICE :	
BOTTLE SIZE :		ALCOHOL :	

COLOR METER

- BLACK
- BARK BROWN
- MAHOGANY
- BRICK
- DARK AMBER
- AMBER
- GOLD
- STRAW
- CLEAR

FLAVOR WHEEL

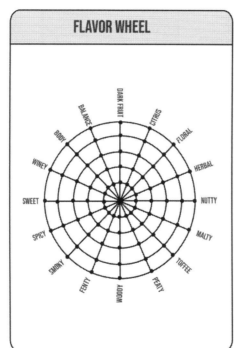

FLAVOR NOTES

FINAL RATING		ADDITIONAL NOTES
APPEARANCE :	☆☆☆☆☆	
TASTE :	☆☆☆☆☆	
MOUTHFEEL :	☆☆☆☆☆	
OVERALL RATING :	☆☆☆☆☆	

BOURBON NAME :		DATE TASTED :	
DISTILLERY :		TYPE / GRADE :	
COUNTRY ORIGIN :		AGE :	
SAMPLED :		PRICE :	
BOTTLE SIZE :		ALCOHOL :	

COLOR METER

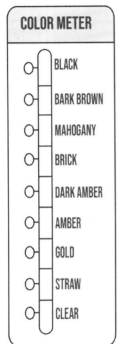

- BLACK
- BARK BROWN
- MAHOGANY
- BRICK
- DARK AMBER
- AMBER
- GOLD
- STRAW
- CLEAR

FLAVOR WHEEL

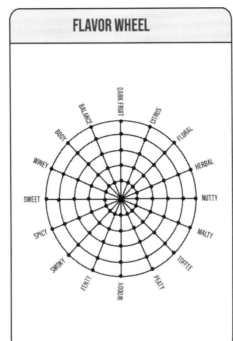

FLAVOR NOTES

FINAL RATING		ADDITIONAL NOTES
APPEARANCE :	☆☆☆☆☆	
TASTE :	☆☆☆☆☆	
MOUTHFEEL :	☆☆☆☆☆	
OVERALL RATING :	☆☆☆☆☆	

BOURBON NAME :		DATE TASTED :	
DISTILLERY :		TYPE / GRADE :	
COUNTRY ORIGIN :		AGE :	
SAMPLED :		PRICE :	
BOTTLE SIZE :		ALCOHOL :	

COLOR METER

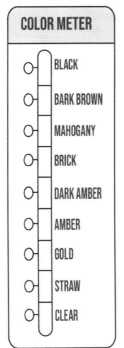

- BLACK
- BARK BROWN
- MAHOGANY
- BRICK
- DARK AMBER
- AMBER
- GOLD
- STRAW
- CLEAR

FLAVOR WHEEL

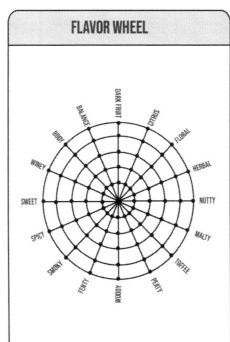

FLAVOR NOTES

FINAL RATING		ADDITIONAL NOTES
APPEARANCE :	☆☆☆☆☆	
TASTE :	☆☆☆☆☆	
MOUTHFEEL :	☆☆☆☆☆	
OVERALL RATING :	☆☆☆☆☆	

BOURBON NAME:		**DATE TASTED:**	
DISTILLERY:		**TYPE / GRADE:**	
COUNTRY ORIGIN:		**AGE:**	
SAMPLED:		**PRICE:**	
BOTTLE SIZE:		**ALCOHOL:**	

COLOR METER

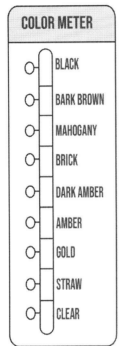

FLAVOR WHEEL

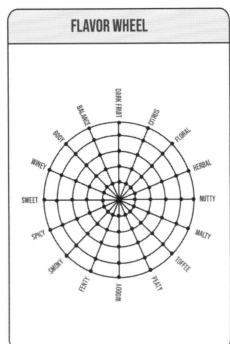

FLAVOR NOTES

FINAL RATING		ADDITIONAL NOTES
APPEARANCE:	☆☆☆☆☆	
TASTE:	☆☆☆☆☆	
MOUTHFEEL:	☆☆☆☆☆	
OVERALL RATING:	☆☆☆☆☆	

BOURBON NAME :		DATE TASTED :	
DISTILLERY :		TYPE / GRADE :	
COUNTRY ORIGIN :		AGE :	
SAMPLED :		PRICE :	
BOTTLE SIZE :		ALCOHOL :	

COLOR METER

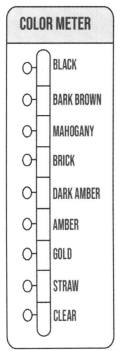

- BLACK
- BARK BROWN
- MAHOGANY
- BRICK
- DARK AMBER
- AMBER
- GOLD
- STRAW
- CLEAR

FLAVOR WHEEL

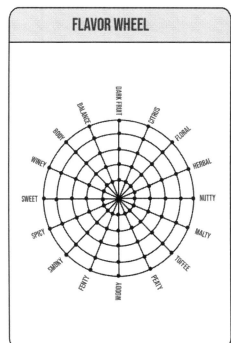

FLAVOR NOTES

FINAL RATING		ADDITIONAL NOTES
APPEARANCE :	☆☆☆☆☆	
TASTE :	☆☆☆☆☆	
MOUTHFEEL :	☆☆☆☆☆	
OVERALL RATING :	☆☆☆☆☆	

🏭 BOURBON NAME :		📅 DATE TASTED :	
🏭 DISTILLERY :		🔭 TYPE / GRADE :	
🌍 COUNTRY ORIGIN :		👥 AGE :	
🧪 SAMPLED :		💲 PRICE :	
🍾 BOTTLE SIZE :		🍶 ALCOHOL :	

COLOR METER

- ○ BLACK
- ○ BARK BROWN
- ○ MAHOGANY
- ○ BRICK
- ○ DARK AMBER
- ○ AMBER
- ○ GOLD
- ○ STRAW
- ○ CLEAR

FLAVOR WHEEL

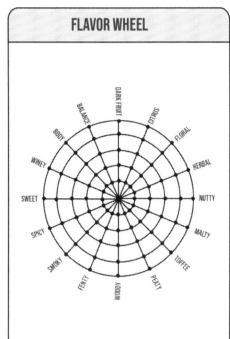

FLAVOR NOTES

FINAL RATING		ADDITIONAL NOTES
🏭 APPEARANCE :	☆☆☆☆☆	
👃 TASTE :	☆☆☆☆☆	
👄 MOUTHFEEL :	☆☆☆☆☆	
🥃 OVERALL RATING :	☆☆☆☆☆	

BOURBON NAME:		**DATE TASTED:**	
DISTILLERY:		**TYPE / GRADE:**	
COUNTRY ORIGIN:		**AGE:**	
SAMPLED:		**PRICE:**	
BOTTLE SIZE:		**ALCOHOL:**	

COLOR METER

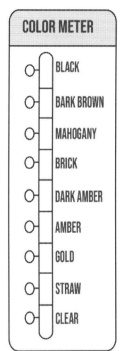

- BLACK
- BARK BROWN
- MAHOGANY
- BRICK
- DARK AMBER
- AMBER
- GOLD
- STRAW
- CLEAR

FLAVOR WHEEL

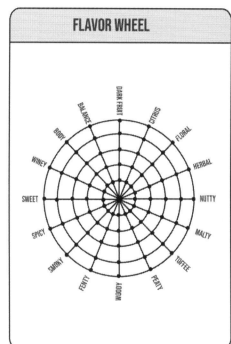

FLAVOR NOTES

FINAL RATING		ADDITIONAL NOTES
APPEARANCE:	☆☆☆☆☆	
TASTE:	☆☆☆☆☆	
MOUTHFEEL:	☆☆☆☆☆	
OVERALL RATING:	☆☆☆☆☆	

BOURBON NAME :		DATE TASTED :	
DISTILLERY :		TYPE / GRADE :	
COUNTRY ORIGIN :		AGE :	
SAMPLED :		PRICE :	
BOTTLE SIZE :		ALCOHOL :	

COLOR METER

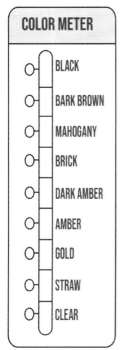

FLAVOR WHEEL

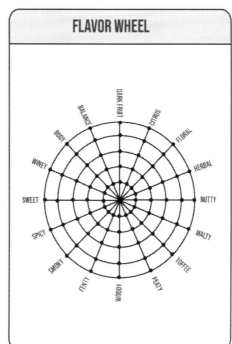

FLAVOR NOTES

FINAL RATING		ADDITIONAL NOTES
APPEARANCE :	☆☆☆☆☆	
TASTE :	☆☆☆☆☆	
MOUTHFEEL :	☆☆☆☆☆	
OVERALL RATING :	☆☆☆☆☆	

BOURBON NAME :		DATE TASTED :	
DISTILLERY :		TYPE / GRADE :	
COUNTRY ORIGIN :		AGE :	
SAMPLED :		PRICE :	
BOTTLE SIZE :		ALCOHOL :	

COLOR METER

- BLACK
- BARK BROWN
- MAHOGANY
- BRICK
- DARK AMBER
- AMBER
- GOLD
- STRAW
- CLEAR

FLAVOR WHEEL

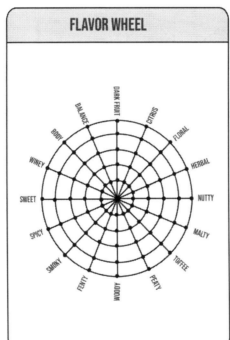

FLAVOR NOTES

FINAL RATING		ADDITIONAL NOTES
APPEARANCE :	☆☆☆☆☆	
TASTE :	☆☆☆☆☆	
MOUTHFEEL :	☆☆☆☆☆	
OVERALL RATING :	☆☆☆☆☆	

BOURBON NAME :		DATE TASTED :	
DISTILLERY :		TYPE / GRADE :	
COUNTRY ORIGIN :		AGE :	
SAMPLED :		PRICE :	
BOTTLE SIZE :		ALCOHOL :	

COLOR METER

- BLACK
- BARK BROWN
- MAHOGANY
- BRICK
- DARK AMBER
- AMBER
- GOLD
- STRAW
- CLEAR

FLAVOR WHEEL

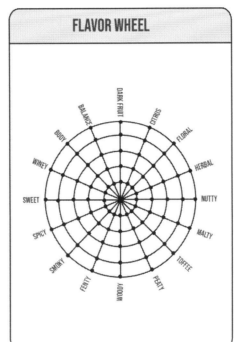

DARK FRUIT, CITRUS, FLORAL, HERBAL, NUTTY, MALTY, TOFFEE, PEATY, WOODY, FRUITY, SMOKY, SPICY, SWEET, WINEY, BODY, BALANCE

FLAVOR NOTES

FINAL RATING		ADDITIONAL NOTES
APPEARANCE :	☆☆☆☆☆	
TASTE :	☆☆☆☆☆	
MOUTHFEEL :	☆☆☆☆☆	
OVERALL RATING :	☆☆☆☆☆	

BOURBON NAME :		DATE TASTED :	
DISTILLERY :		TYPE / GRADE :	
COUNTRY ORIGIN :		AGE :	
SAMPLED :		PRICE :	
BOTTLE SIZE :		ALCOHOL :	

COLOR METER

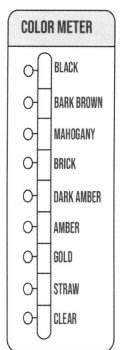

- BLACK
- BARK BROWN
- MAHOGANY
- BRICK
- DARK AMBER
- AMBER
- GOLD
- STRAW
- CLEAR

FLAVOR WHEEL

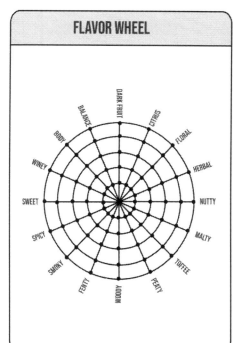

FLAVOR NOTES

FINAL RATING		ADDITIONAL NOTES
APPEARANCE :	☆☆☆☆☆	
TASTE :	☆☆☆☆☆	
MOUTHFEEL :	☆☆☆☆☆	
OVERALL RATING :	☆☆☆☆☆	

🍾 BOURBON NAME :		📅 DATE TASTED :	
🏭 DISTILLERY :		🔬 TYPE / GRADE :	
🌐 COUNTRY ORIGIN :		👥 AGE :	
🧪 SAMPLED :		💰 PRICE :	
🍼 BOTTLE SIZE :		🥃 ALCOHOL :	

COLOR METER

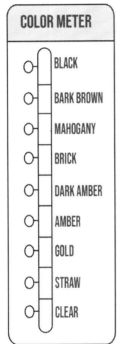

FLAVOR WHEEL

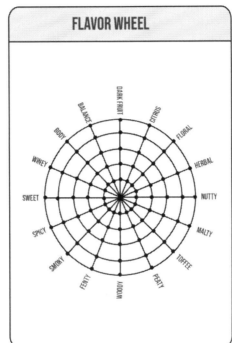

FLAVOR NOTES

FINAL RATING		ADDITIONAL NOTES
🏭 APPEARANCE :	☆☆☆☆☆	
👃 TASTE :	☆☆☆☆☆	
👄 MOUTHFEEL :	☆☆☆☆☆	
🏆 OVERALL RATING :	☆☆☆☆☆	

BOURBON NAME :		DATE TASTED :	
DISTILLERY :		TYPE / GRADE :	
COUNTRY ORIGIN :		AGE :	
SAMPLED :		PRICE :	
BOTTLE SIZE :		ALCOHOL :	

COLOR METER	FLAVOR WHEEL	FLAVOR NOTES
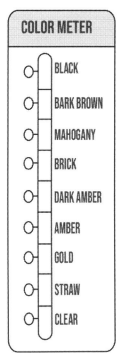	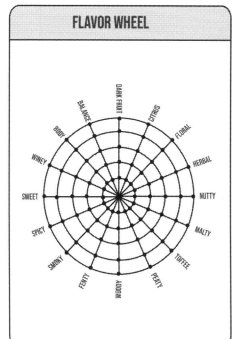	

FINAL RATING		ADDITIONAL NOTES
APPEARANCE :	☆☆☆☆☆	
TASTE :	☆☆☆☆☆	
MOUTHFEEL :	☆☆☆☆☆	
OVERALL RATING :	☆☆☆☆☆	

BOURBON NAME :		DATE TASTED :	
DISTILLERY :		TYPE / GRADE :	
COUNTRY ORIGIN :		AGE :	
SAMPLED :		PRICE :	
BOTTLE SIZE :		ALCOHOL :	

COLOR METER	FLAVOR WHEEL	FLAVOR NOTES
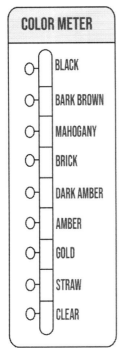	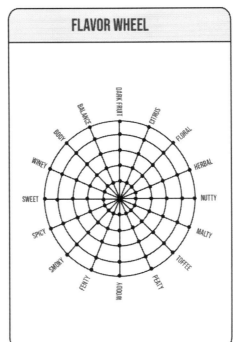	

FINAL RATING | ADDITIONAL NOTES

APPEARANCE :	☆☆☆☆☆	
TASTE :	☆☆☆☆☆	
MOUTHFEEL :	☆☆☆☆☆	
OVERALL RATING :	☆☆☆☆☆	

BOURBON NAME:		**DATE TASTED:**	
DISTILLERY:		**TYPE / GRADE:**	
COUNTRY ORIGIN:		**AGE:**	
SAMPLED:		**PRICE:**	
BOTTLE SIZE:		**ALCOHOL:**	

COLOR METER

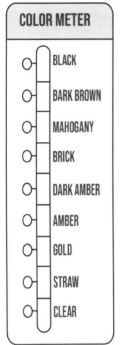

FLAVOR WHEEL

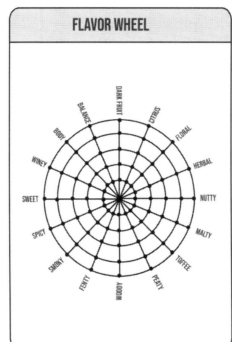

FLAVOR NOTES

FINAL RATING		ADDITIONAL NOTES
APPEARANCE:	☆☆☆☆☆	
TASTE:	☆☆☆☆☆	
MOUTHFEEL:	☆☆☆☆☆	
OVERALL RATING:	☆☆☆☆☆	

BOURBON NAME :		DATE TASTED :	
DISTILLERY :		TYPE / GRADE :	
COUNTRY ORIGIN :		AGE :	
SAMPLED :		PRICE :	
BOTTLE SIZE :		ALCOHOL :	

COLOR METER

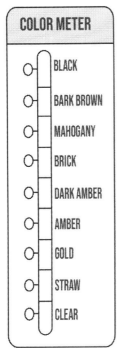

- BLACK
- BARK BROWN
- MAHOGANY
- BRICK
- DARK AMBER
- AMBER
- GOLD
- STRAW
- CLEAR

FLAVOR WHEEL

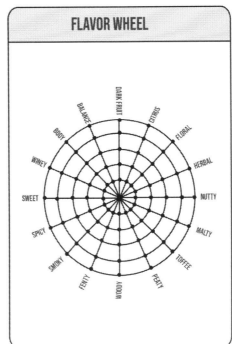

FLAVOR NOTES

FINAL RATING		ADDITIONAL NOTES
APPEARANCE :	☆☆☆☆☆	
TASTE :	☆☆☆☆☆	
MOUTHFEEL :	☆☆☆☆☆	
OVERALL RATING :	☆☆☆☆☆	

BOURBON NAME :		DATE TASTED :	
DISTILLERY :		TYPE / GRADE :	
COUNTRY ORIGIN :		AGE :	
SAMPLED :		PRICE :	
BOTTLE SIZE :		ALCOHOL :	

COLOR METER

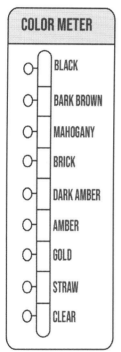

- BLACK
- BARK BROWN
- MAHOGANY
- BRICK
- DARK AMBER
- AMBER
- GOLD
- STRAW
- CLEAR

FLAVOR WHEEL

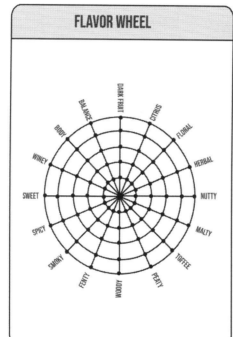

FLAVOR NOTES

FINAL RATING		ADDITIONAL NOTES
APPEARANCE :	☆☆☆☆☆	
TASTE :	☆☆☆☆☆	
MOUTHFEEL :	☆☆☆☆☆	
OVERALL RATING :	☆☆☆☆☆	

🏭 BOURBON NAME :		📅 DATE TASTED :	
🏺 DISTILLERY :		🔭 TYPE / GRADE :	
🌍 COUNTRY ORIGIN :		👥 AGE :	
🧪 SAMPLED :		💰 PRICE :	
🍾 BOTTLE SIZE :		🥃 ALCOHOL :	

COLOR METER

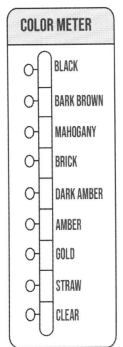

FLAVOR WHEEL

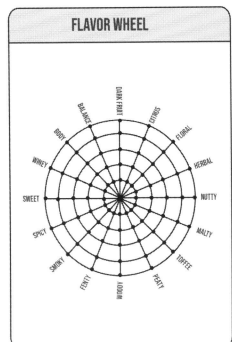

FLAVOR NOTES

FINAL RATING		ADDITIONAL NOTES
🏭 APPEARANCE :	☆☆☆☆☆	
👃 TASTE :	☆☆☆☆☆	
👄 MOUTHFEEL :	☆☆☆☆☆	
🥃 OVERALL RATING :	☆☆☆☆☆	

🍾 BOURBON NAME :		📅 DATE TASTED :	
🏭 DISTILLERY :		🧪 TYPE / GRADE :	
🌍 COUNTRY ORIGIN :		👥 AGE :	
🖊 SAMPLED :		🏷 PRICE :	
🍼 BOTTLE SIZE :		🥃 ALCOHOL :	

COLOR METER

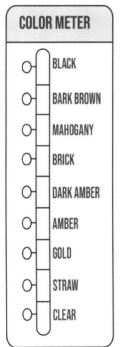

- BLACK
- BARK BROWN
- MAHOGANY
- BRICK
- DARK AMBER
- AMBER
- GOLD
- STRAW
- CLEAR

FLAVOR WHEEL

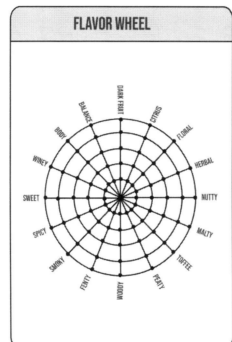

FLAVOR NOTES

FINAL RATING		ADDITIONAL NOTES
🏭 APPEARANCE :	☆☆☆☆☆	
👃 TASTE :	☆☆☆☆☆	
👄 MOUTHFEEL :	☆☆☆☆☆	
🏆 OVERALL RATING :	☆☆☆☆☆	

BOURBON NAME :		DATE TASTED :	
DISTILLERY :		TYPE / GRADE :	
COUNTRY ORIGIN :		AGE :	
SAMPLED :		PRICE :	
BOTTLE SIZE :		ALCOHOL :	

COLOR METER

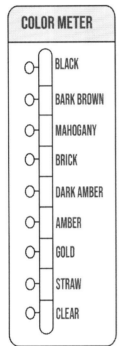

- BLACK
- BARK BROWN
- MAHOGANY
- BRICK
- DARK AMBER
- AMBER
- GOLD
- STRAW
- CLEAR

FLAVOR WHEEL

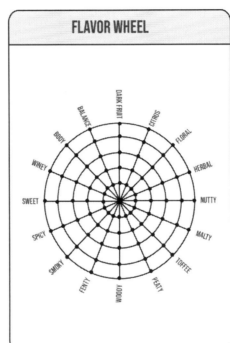

FLAVOR NOTES

FINAL RATING		ADDITIONAL NOTES
APPEARANCE :	☆☆☆☆☆	
TASTE :	☆☆☆☆☆	
MOUTHFEEL :	☆☆☆☆☆	
OVERALL RATING :	☆☆☆☆☆	

BOURBON NAME :		DATE TASTED :	
DISTILLERY :		TYPE / GRADE :	
COUNTRY ORIGIN :		AGE :	
SAMPLED :		PRICE :	
BOTTLE SIZE :		ALCOHOL :	

COLOR METER

- BLACK
- BARK BROWN
- MAHOGANY
- BRICK
- DARK AMBER
- AMBER
- GOLD
- STRAW
- CLEAR

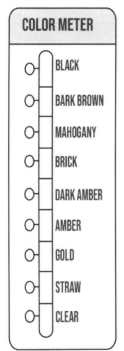

FLAVOR WHEEL

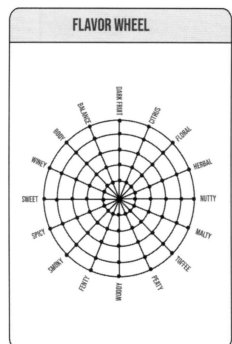

FLAVOR NOTES

FINAL RATING		ADDITIONAL NOTES
APPEARANCE :	☆☆☆☆☆	
TASTE :	☆☆☆☆☆	
MOUTHFEEL :	☆☆☆☆☆	
OVERALL RATING :	☆☆☆☆☆	

BOURBON NAME :		DATE TASTED :	
DISTILLERY :		TYPE / GRADE :	
COUNTRY ORIGIN :		AGE :	
SAMPLED :		PRICE :	
BOTTLE SIZE :		ALCOHOL :	

COLOR METER / FLAVOR WHEEL / FLAVOR NOTES

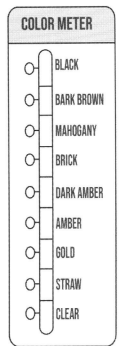
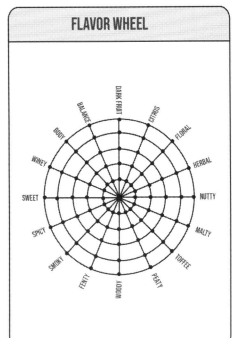

FINAL RATING		ADDITIONAL NOTES
APPEARANCE :	☆☆☆☆☆	
TASTE :	☆☆☆☆☆	
MOUTHFEEL :	☆☆☆☆☆	
OVERALL RATING :	☆☆☆☆☆	

🥃 BOURBON NAME :		📅 DATE TASTED :	
🏭 DISTILLERY :		🔭 TYPE / GRADE :	
🌐 COUNTRY ORIGIN :		👥 AGE :	
🧪 SAMPLED :		🏷️ PRICE :	
🍾 BOTTLE SIZE :		🍶 ALCOHOL :	

COLOR METER

- ○ BLACK
- ○ BARK BROWN
- ○ MAHOGANY
- ○ BRICK
- ○ DARK AMBER
- ○ AMBER
- ○ GOLD
- ○ STRAW
- ○ CLEAR

FLAVOR WHEEL

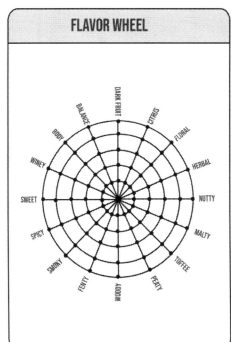

FLAVOR NOTES

FINAL RATING		ADDITIONAL NOTES
🥃 APPEARANCE :	☆☆☆☆☆	
👃 TASTE :	☆☆☆☆☆	
👄 MOUTHFEEL :	☆☆☆☆☆	
🌟 OVERALL RATING :	☆☆☆☆☆	

🏭 BOURBON NAME :		📅 DATE TASTED :	
🏷️ DISTILLERY :		⚗️ TYPE / GRADE :	
🌐 COUNTRY ORIGIN :		👤 AGE :	
✒️ SAMPLED :		💲 PRICE :	
🍾 BOTTLE SIZE :		🥃 ALCOHOL :	

COLOR METER

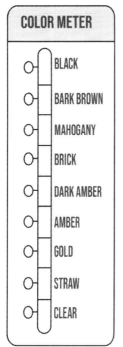

FLAVOR WHEEL

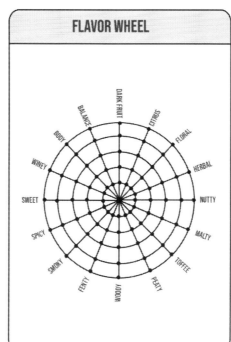

FLAVOR NOTES

FINAL RATING		ADDITIONAL NOTES
🏠 APPEARANCE :	☆☆☆☆☆	
👃 TASTE :	☆☆☆☆☆	
👄 MOUTHFEEL :	☆☆☆☆☆	
🏆 OVERALL RATING :	☆☆☆☆☆	

🍾 BOURBON NAME :		📅 DATE TASTED :	
🏭 DISTILLERY :		🔭 TYPE / GRADE :	
🌍 COUNTRY ORIGIN :		👥 AGE :	
💧 SAMPLED :		💰 PRICE :	
🍾 BOTTLE SIZE :		🥃 ALCOHOL :	

COLOR METER

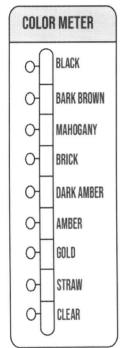

- BLACK
- BARK BROWN
- MAHOGANY
- BRICK
- DARK AMBER
- AMBER
- GOLD
- STRAW
- CLEAR

FLAVOR WHEEL

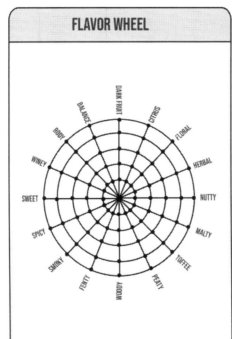

FLAVOR NOTES

FINAL RATING		ADDITIONAL NOTES
🍾 APPEARANCE :	☆☆☆☆☆	
👃 TASTE :	☆☆☆☆☆	
👄 MOUTHFEEL :	☆☆☆☆☆	
⭐ OVERALL RATING :	☆☆☆☆☆	

BOURBON NAME:		**DATE TASTED:**	
DISTILLERY:		**TYPE / GRADE:**	
COUNTRY ORIGIN:		**AGE:**	
SAMPLED:		**PRICE:**	
BOTTLE SIZE:		**ALCOHOL:**	

COLOR METER

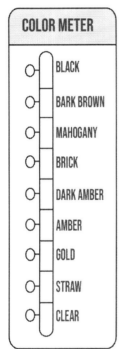

FLAVOR WHEEL

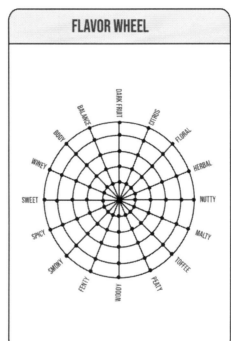

FLAVOR NOTES

FINAL RATING | ADDITIONAL NOTES

APPEARANCE:	☆☆☆☆☆	
TASTE:	☆☆☆☆☆	
MOUTHFEEL:	☆☆☆☆☆	
OVERALL RATING:	☆☆☆☆☆	

BOURBON NAME :		DATE TASTED :	
DISTILLERY :		TYPE / GRADE :	
COUNTRY ORIGIN :		AGE :	
SAMPLED :		PRICE :	
BOTTLE SIZE :		ALCOHOL :	

COLOR METER

- BLACK
- BARK BROWN
- MAHOGANY
- BRICK
- DARK AMBER
- AMBER
- GOLD
- STRAW
- CLEAR

FLAVOR WHEEL

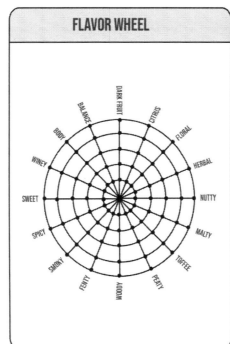

DARK FRUIT, CITRUS, FLORAL, HERBAL, NUTTY, MALTY, TOFFEE, PEATY, WOODY, FENTY, SMOKY, SPICY, SWEET, WINEY, BODY, BALANCE

FLAVOR NOTES

FINAL RATING		ADDITIONAL NOTES
APPEARANCE :	☆☆☆☆☆	
TASTE :	☆☆☆☆☆	
MOUTHFEEL :	☆☆☆☆☆	
OVERALL RATING :	☆☆☆☆☆	

BOURBON NAME:		**DATE TASTED:**	
DISTILLERY:		**TYPE / GRADE:**	
COUNTRY ORIGIN:		**AGE:**	
SAMPLED:		**PRICE:**	
BOTTLE SIZE:		**ALCOHOL:**	

COLOR METER

- BLACK
- BARK BROWN
- MAHOGANY
- BRICK
- DARK AMBER
- AMBER
- GOLD
- STRAW
- CLEAR

FLAVOR WHEEL

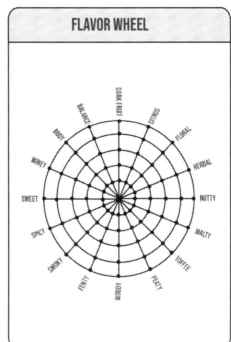

FLAVOR NOTES

FINAL RATING		ADDITIONAL NOTES
APPEARANCE:	☆☆☆☆☆	
TASTE:	☆☆☆☆☆	
MOUTHFEEL:	☆☆☆☆☆	
OVERALL RATING:	☆☆☆☆☆	

BOURBON NAME:		DATE TASTED:	
DISTILLERY:		TYPE / GRADE:	
COUNTRY ORIGIN:		AGE:	
SAMPLED:		PRICE:	
BOTTLE SIZE:		ALCOHOL:	

COLOR METER

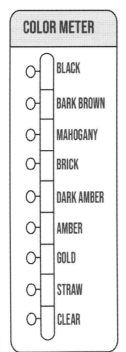

- BLACK
- BARK BROWN
- MAHOGANY
- BRICK
- DARK AMBER
- AMBER
- GOLD
- STRAW
- CLEAR

FLAVOR WHEEL

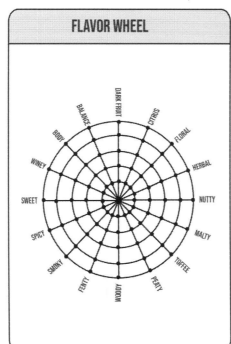

BALANCE, DARK FRUIT, CITRUS, FLORAL, HERBAL, NUTTY, MALTY, TOFFEE, PEATY, WOODY, FENTY, SMOKY, SPICY, SWEET, WINEY, BODY

FLAVOR NOTES

FINAL RATING		ADDITIONAL NOTES
APPEARANCE:	☆☆☆☆☆	
TASTE:	☆☆☆☆☆	
MOUTHFEEL:	☆☆☆☆☆	
OVERALL RATING:	☆☆☆☆☆	

BOURBON NAME :		DATE TASTED :	
DISTILLERY :		TYPE / GRADE :	
COUNTRY ORIGIN :		AGE :	
SAMPLED :		PRICE :	
BOTTLE SIZE :		ALCOHOL :	

COLOR METER

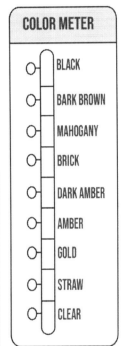

- BLACK
- BARK BROWN
- MAHOGANY
- BRICK
- DARK AMBER
- AMBER
- GOLD
- STRAW
- CLEAR

FLAVOR WHEEL

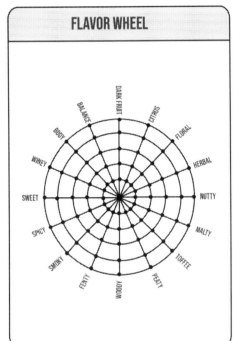

FLAVOR NOTES

FINAL RATING | ADDITIONAL NOTES

APPEARANCE :	☆☆☆☆☆	
TASTE :	☆☆☆☆☆	
MOUTHFEEL :	☆☆☆☆☆	
OVERALL RATING :	☆☆☆☆☆	

🍾 BOURBON NAME :		📅 DATE TASTED :	
🏭 DISTILLERY :		🍾 TYPE / GRADE :	
🌍 COUNTRY ORIGIN :		👥 AGE :	
🧪 SAMPLED :		🏷️ PRICE :	
🍾 BOTTLE SIZE :		🥃 ALCOHOL :	

COLOR METER

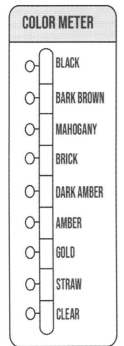

FLAVOR WHEEL

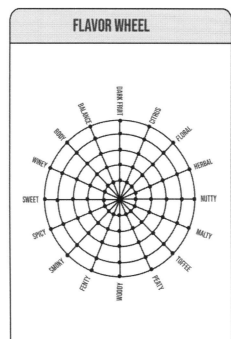

FLAVOR NOTES

FINAL RATING		ADDITIONAL NOTES
🍾 APPEARANCE :	☆☆☆☆☆	
👃 TASTE :	☆☆☆☆☆	
👄 MOUTHFEEL :	☆☆☆☆☆	
🏆 OVERALL RATING :	☆☆☆☆☆	

BOURBON NAME :		**DATE TASTED :**	
DISTILLERY :		**TYPE / GRADE :**	
COUNTRY ORIGIN :		**AGE :**	
SAMPLED :		**PRICE :**	
BOTTLE SIZE :		**ALCOHOL :**	

COLOR METER

- BLACK
- BARK BROWN
- MAHOGANY
- BRICK
- DARK AMBER
- AMBER
- GOLD
- STRAW
- CLEAR

FLAVOR WHEEL

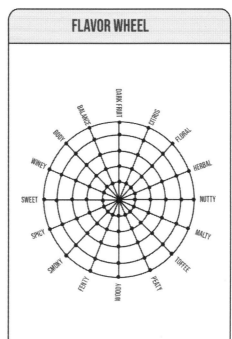

DARK FRUIT, CITRUS, FLORAL, HERBAL, NUTTY, MALTY, TOFFEE, PEATY, WOODY, FRUITY, SMOKY, SPICY, SWEET, WINEY, BODY, BALANCE

FLAVOR NOTES

FINAL RATING		ADDITIONAL NOTES
APPEARANCE :	☆☆☆☆☆	
TASTE :	☆☆☆☆☆	
MOUTHFEEL :	☆☆☆☆☆	
OVERALL RATING :	☆☆☆☆☆	

BOURBON NAME :		DATE TASTED :	
DISTILLERY :		TYPE / GRADE :	
COUNTRY ORIGIN :		AGE :	
SAMPLED :		PRICE :	
BOTTLE SIZE :		ALCOHOL :	

COLOR METER

- BLACK
- BARK BROWN
- MAHOGANY
- BRICK
- DARK AMBER
- AMBER
- GOLD
- STRAW
- CLEAR

FLAVOR WHEEL

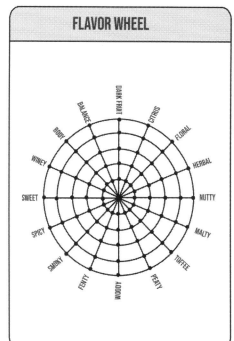

FLAVOR NOTES

FINAL RATING		ADDITIONAL NOTES
APPEARANCE :	☆☆☆☆☆	
TASTE :	☆☆☆☆☆	
MOUTHFEEL :	☆☆☆☆☆	
OVERALL RATING :	☆☆☆☆☆	

BOURBON NAME :		**DATE TASTED :**	
DISTILLERY :		**TYPE / GRADE :**	
COUNTRY ORIGIN :		**AGE :**	
SAMPLED :		**PRICE :**	
BOTTLE SIZE :		**ALCOHOL :**	

COLOR METER

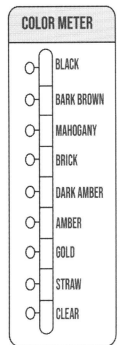

- BLACK
- BARK BROWN
- MAHOGANY
- BRICK
- DARK AMBER
- AMBER
- GOLD
- STRAW
- CLEAR

FLAVOR WHEEL

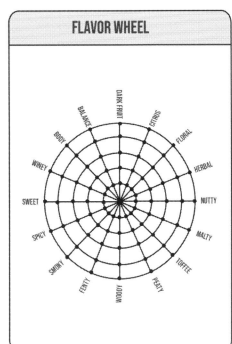

FLAVOR NOTES

FINAL RATING		ADDITIONAL NOTES
APPEARANCE :	☆☆☆☆☆	
TASTE :	☆☆☆☆☆	
MOUTHFEEL :	☆☆☆☆☆	
OVERALL RATING :	☆☆☆☆☆	

🍾 BOURBON NAME :		📅 DATE TASTED :	
🏭 DISTILLERY :		🔍 TYPE / GRADE :	
🌐 COUNTRY ORIGIN :		👥 AGE :	
🥃 SAMPLED :		🏷️ PRICE :	
🍾 BOTTLE SIZE :		🧪 ALCOHOL :	

COLOR METER

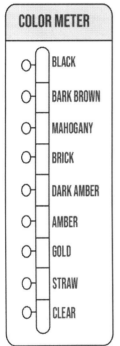

- BLACK
- BARK BROWN
- MAHOGANY
- BRICK
- DARK AMBER
- AMBER
- GOLD
- STRAW
- CLEAR

FLAVOR WHEEL

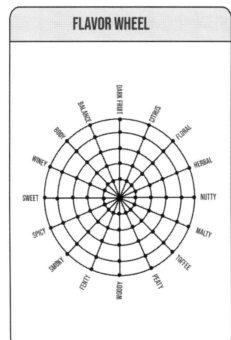

FLAVOR NOTES

FINAL RATING		ADDITIONAL NOTES
🍾 APPEARANCE :	☆☆☆☆☆	
👃 TASTE :	☆☆☆☆☆	
👄 MOUTHFEEL :	☆☆☆☆☆	
🏆 OVERALL RATING :	☆☆☆☆☆	

BOURBON NAME :		**DATE TASTED :**	
DISTILLERY :		**TYPE / GRADE :**	
COUNTRY ORIGIN :		**AGE :**	
SAMPLED :		**PRICE :**	
BOTTLE SIZE :		**ALCOHOL :**	

COLOR METER

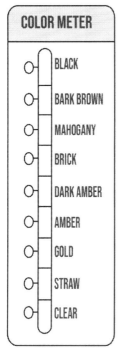

FLAVOR WHEEL

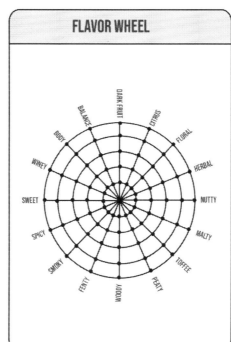

FLAVOR NOTES

FINAL RATING		ADDITIONAL NOTES
APPEARANCE :	☆☆☆☆☆	
TASTE :	☆☆☆☆☆	
MOUTHFEEL :	☆☆☆☆☆	
OVERALL RATING :	☆☆☆☆☆	

BOURBON NAME :		**DATE TASTED :**	
DISTILLERY :		**TYPE / GRADE :**	
COUNTRY ORIGIN :		**AGE :**	
SAMPLED :		**PRICE :**	
BOTTLE SIZE :		**ALCOHOL :**	

COLOR METER

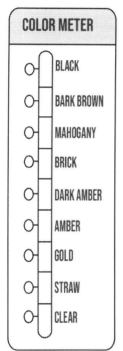

- BLACK
- BARK BROWN
- MAHOGANY
- BRICK
- DARK AMBER
- AMBER
- GOLD
- STRAW
- CLEAR

FLAVOR WHEEL

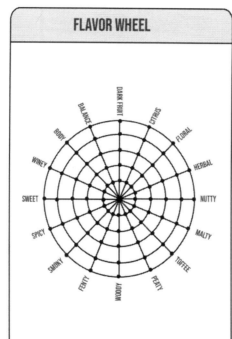

FLAVOR NOTES

FINAL RATING		ADDITIONAL NOTES
APPEARANCE :	☆☆☆☆☆	
TASTE :	☆☆☆☆☆	
MOUTHFEEL :	☆☆☆☆☆	
OVERALL RATING :	☆☆☆☆☆	

🏭 BOURBON NAME :		📅 DATE TASTED :	
🧪 DISTILLERY :		🧪 TYPE / GRADE :	
🌍 COUNTRY ORIGIN :		👥 AGE :	
🧪 SAMPLED :		🏷️ PRICE :	
🍾 BOTTLE SIZE :		🍶 ALCOHOL :	

COLOR METER

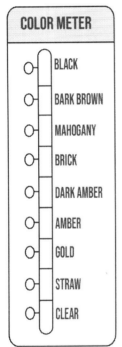

- BLACK
- BARK BROWN
- MAHOGANY
- BRICK
- DARK AMBER
- AMBER
- GOLD
- STRAW
- CLEAR

FLAVOR WHEEL

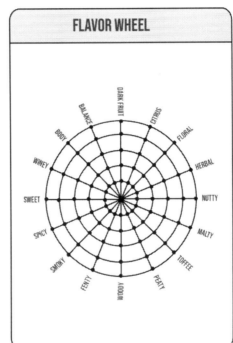

DARK FRUIT, CITRUS, FLORAL, HERBAL, NUTTY, MALTY, TOFFEE, PEATY, WOODY, PEATY, SMOKY, SPICY, SWEET, WINEY, BODY, BALANCE

FLAVOR NOTES

FINAL RATING		ADDITIONAL NOTES
🏭 APPEARANCE :	☆☆☆☆☆	
👃 TASTE :	☆☆☆☆☆	
👄 MOUTHFEEL :	☆☆☆☆☆	
🏆 OVERALL RATING :	☆☆☆☆☆	

BOURBON NAME :		DATE TASTED :	
DISTILLERY :		TYPE / GRADE :	
COUNTRY ORIGIN :		AGE :	
SAMPLED :		PRICE :	
BOTTLE SIZE :		ALCOHOL :	

COLOR METER

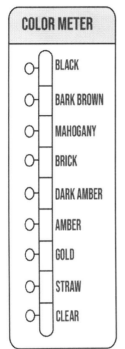

- BLACK
- BARK BROWN
- MAHOGANY
- BRICK
- DARK AMBER
- AMBER
- GOLD
- STRAW
- CLEAR

FLAVOR WHEEL

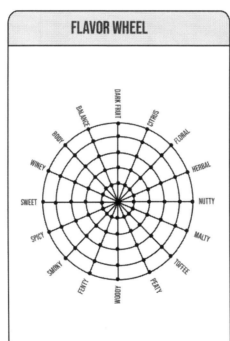

FLAVOR NOTES

FINAL RATING		ADDITIONAL NOTES
APPEARANCE :	☆☆☆☆☆	
TASTE :	☆☆☆☆☆	
MOUTHFEEL :	☆☆☆☆☆	
OVERALL RATING :	☆☆☆☆☆	

BOURBON NAME :		DATE TASTED :	
DISTILLERY :		TYPE / GRADE :	
COUNTRY ORIGIN :		AGE :	
SAMPLED :		PRICE :	
BOTTLE SIZE :		ALCOHOL :	

COLOR METER

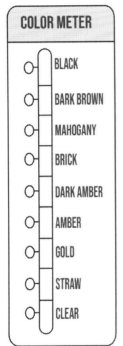

- BLACK
- BARK BROWN
- MAHOGANY
- BRICK
- DARK AMBER
- AMBER
- GOLD
- STRAW
- CLEAR

FLAVOR WHEEL

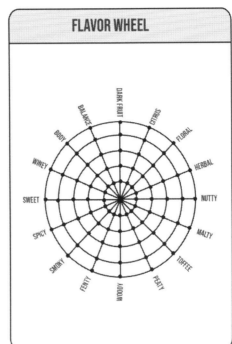

FLAVOR NOTES

FINAL RATING		ADDITIONAL NOTES
APPEARANCE :	☆☆☆☆☆	
TASTE :	☆☆☆☆☆	
MOUTHFEEL :	☆☆☆☆☆	
OVERALL RATING :	☆☆☆☆☆	

🍾 BOURBON NAME :		📅 DATE TASTED :	
🏭 DISTILLERY :		🔬 TYPE / GRADE :	
🌍 COUNTRY ORIGIN :		👥 AGE :	
🧪 SAMPLED :		💲 PRICE :	
🍾 BOTTLE SIZE :		🥃 ALCOHOL :	

COLOR METER

- BLACK
- BARK BROWN
- MAHOGANY
- BRICK
- DARK AMBER
- AMBER
- GOLD
- STRAW
- CLEAR

FLAVOR WHEEL

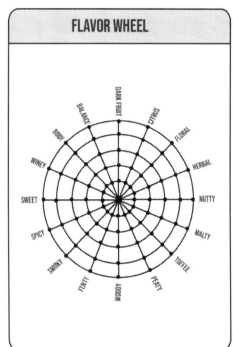

FLAVOR NOTES

FINAL RATING		ADDITIONAL NOTES
🍺 APPEARANCE :	☆☆☆☆☆	
👃 TASTE :	☆☆☆☆☆	
👄 MOUTHFEEL :	☆☆☆☆☆	
🏆 OVERALL RATING :	☆☆☆☆☆	

BOURBON NAME:		**DATE TASTED:**	
DISTILLERY:		**TYPE / GRADE:**	
COUNTRY ORIGIN:		**AGE:**	
SAMPLED:		**PRICE:**	
BOTTLE SIZE:		**ALCOHOL:**	

COLOR METER

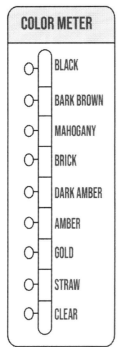

- BLACK
- BARK BROWN
- MAHOGANY
- BRICK
- DARK AMBER
- AMBER
- GOLD
- STRAW
- CLEAR

FLAVOR WHEEL

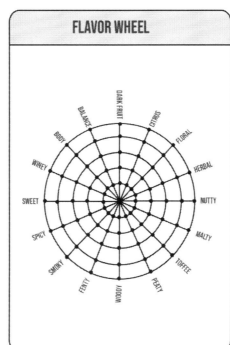

DARK FRUIT, CITRUS, FLORAL, HERBAL, NUTTY, MALTY, TOFFEE, PEATY, WOODY, PEATY, SMOKY, SPICY, SWEET, WINEY, BODY, BALANCE

FLAVOR NOTES

FINAL RATING		ADDITIONAL NOTES
APPEARANCE:	☆☆☆☆☆	
TASTE:	☆☆☆☆☆	
MOUTHFEEL:	☆☆☆☆☆	
OVERALL RATING:	☆☆☆☆☆	

🍾 BOURBON NAME :		📅 DATE TASTED :	
🏭 DISTILLERY :		⚗️ TYPE / GRADE :	
🌍 COUNTRY ORIGIN :		👥 AGE :	
🧪 SAMPLED :		🏷️ PRICE :	
🍾 BOTTLE SIZE :		🍶 ALCOHOL :	

COLOR METER

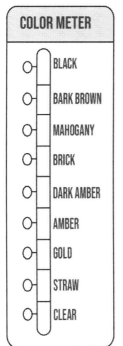

- BLACK
- BARK BROWN
- MAHOGANY
- BRICK
- DARK AMBER
- AMBER
- GOLD
- STRAW
- CLEAR

FLAVOR WHEEL

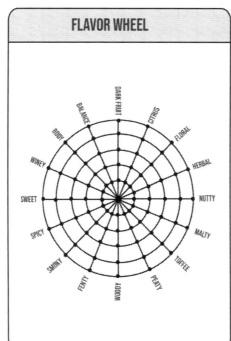

DARK FRUIT, CITRUS, FLORAL, HERBAL, NUTTY, MALTY, TOFFEE, PEATY, WOODY, FENTY, SMOKY, SPICY, SWEET, WINEY, BODY, BALANCE

FLAVOR NOTES

FINAL RATING		ADDITIONAL NOTES
🛢️ APPEARANCE :	☆☆☆☆☆	
👄 TASTE :	☆☆☆☆☆	
👄 MOUTHFEEL :	☆☆☆☆☆	
🏆 OVERALL RATING :	☆☆☆☆☆	

BOURBON NAME :		DATE TASTED :	
DISTILLERY :		TYPE / GRADE :	
COUNTRY ORIGIN :		AGE :	
SAMPLED :		PRICE :	
BOTTLE SIZE :		ALCOHOL :	

COLOR METER

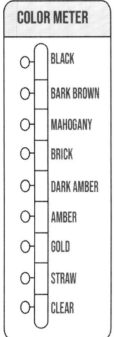

- BLACK
- BARK BROWN
- MAHOGANY
- BRICK
- DARK AMBER
- AMBER
- GOLD
- STRAW
- CLEAR

FLAVOR WHEEL

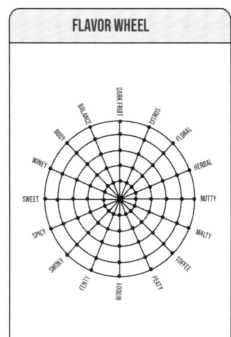

FLAVOR NOTES

FINAL RATING | ADDITIONAL NOTES

APPEARANCE :	☆☆☆☆☆	
TASTE :	☆☆☆☆☆	
MOUTHFEEL :	☆☆☆☆☆	
OVERALL RATING :	☆☆☆☆☆	

🍾 BOURBON NAME :		📅 DATE TASTED :	
🏭 DISTILLERY :		🔬 TYPE / GRADE :	
🌐 COUNTRY ORIGIN :		👥 AGE :	
💧 SAMPLED :		🏷️ PRICE :	
🍶 BOTTLE SIZE :		🍷 ALCOHOL :	

COLOR METER

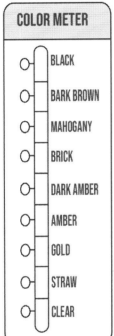

- BLACK
- BARK BROWN
- MAHOGANY
- BRICK
- DARK AMBER
- AMBER
- GOLD
- STRAW
- CLEAR

FLAVOR WHEEL

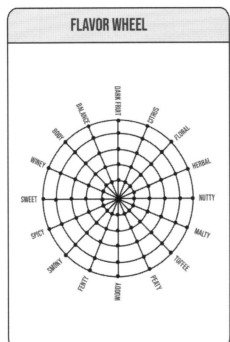

FLAVOR NOTES

FINAL RATING		ADDITIONAL NOTES
🏛️ APPEARANCE :	☆☆☆☆☆	
👅 TASTE :	☆☆☆☆☆	
👄 MOUTHFEEL :	☆☆☆☆☆	
🏆 OVERALL RATING :	☆☆☆☆☆	

BOURBON NAME :		DATE TASTED :	
DISTILLERY :		TYPE / GRADE :	
COUNTRY ORIGIN :		AGE :	
SAMPLED :		PRICE :	
BOTTLE SIZE :		ALCOHOL :	

COLOR METER

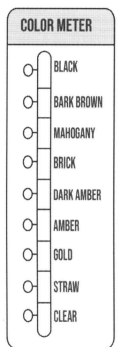

- BLACK
- BARK BROWN
- MAHOGANY
- BRICK
- DARK AMBER
- AMBER
- GOLD
- STRAW
- CLEAR

FLAVOR WHEEL

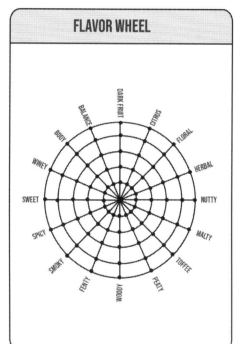

FLAVOR NOTES

FINAL RATING		ADDITIONAL NOTES
APPEARANCE :	☆☆☆☆☆	
TASTE :	☆☆☆☆☆	
MOUTHFEEL :	☆☆☆☆☆	
OVERALL RATING :	☆☆☆☆☆	

BOURBON NAME :		DATE TASTED :	
DISTILLERY :		TYPE / GRADE :	
COUNTRY ORIGIN :		AGE :	
SAMPLED :		PRICE :	
BOTTLE SIZE :		ALCOHOL :	

COLOR METER

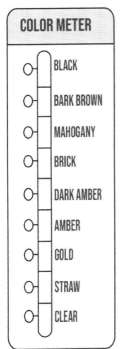

FLAVOR WHEEL

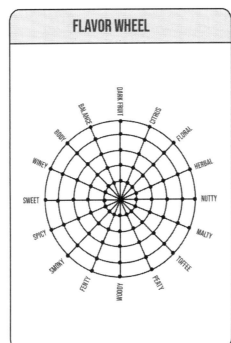

FLAVOR NOTES

FINAL RATING | ADDITIONAL NOTES

FINAL RATING		ADDITIONAL NOTES
APPEARANCE :	☆☆☆☆☆	
TASTE :	☆☆☆☆☆	
MOUTHFEEL :	☆☆☆☆☆	
OVERALL RATING :	☆☆☆☆☆	

🏭 BOURBON NAME :		📅 DATE TASTED :	
🏺 DISTILLERY :		🧪 TYPE / GRADE :	
🌍 COUNTRY ORIGIN :		👥 AGE :	
🧪 SAMPLED :		🏷️ PRICE :	
🍾 BOTTLE SIZE :		🥃 ALCOHOL :	

COLOR METER

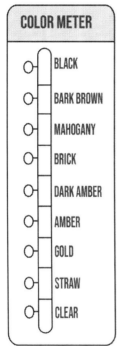

- BLACK
- BARK BROWN
- MAHOGANY
- BRICK
- DARK AMBER
- AMBER
- GOLD
- STRAW
- CLEAR

FLAVOR WHEEL

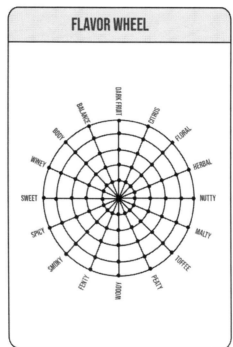

DARK FRUIT, CITRUS, FLORAL, HERBAL, NUTTY, MALTY, TOFFEE, PEATY, WOODY, FRUITY, SMOKY, SPICY, SWEET, WINEY, BODY, BALANCE

FLAVOR NOTES

FINAL RATING		ADDITIONAL NOTES
🏭 APPEARANCE :	☆☆☆☆☆	
👃 TASTE :	☆☆☆☆☆	
👄 MOUTHFEEL :	☆☆☆☆☆	
🏆 OVERALL RATING :	☆☆☆☆☆	

BOURBON NAME :		DATE TASTED :	
DISTILLERY :		TYPE / GRADE :	
COUNTRY ORIGIN :		AGE :	
SAMPLED :		PRICE :	
BOTTLE SIZE :		ALCOHOL :	

COLOR METER

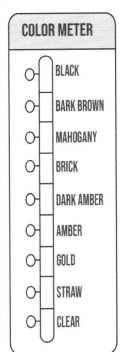

- BLACK
- BARK BROWN
- MAHOGANY
- BRICK
- DARK AMBER
- AMBER
- GOLD
- STRAW
- CLEAR

FLAVOR WHEEL

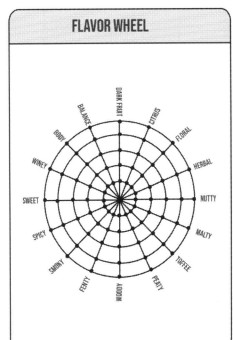

DARK FRUIT, CITRUS, FLORAL, HERBAL, NUTTY, MALTY, TOFFEE, PEATY, AROMA, FENTY, SMOKY, SPICY, SWEET, WINEY, BODY, BALANCE

FLAVOR NOTES

FINAL RATING		ADDITIONAL NOTES
APPEARANCE :	☆☆☆☆☆	
TASTE :	☆☆☆☆☆	
MOUTHFEEL :	☆☆☆☆☆	
OVERALL RATING :	☆☆☆☆☆	

BOURBON NAME :		DATE TASTED :	
DISTILLERY :		TYPE / GRADE :	
COUNTRY ORIGIN :		AGE :	
SAMPLED :		PRICE :	
BOTTLE SIZE :		ALCOHOL :	

COLOR METER

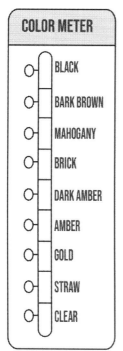

- BLACK
- BARK BROWN
- MAHOGANY
- BRICK
- DARK AMBER
- AMBER
- GOLD
- STRAW
- CLEAR

FLAVOR WHEEL

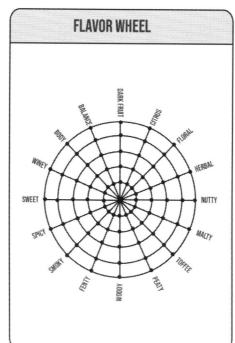

FLAVOR NOTES

FINAL RATING

APPEARANCE :	☆☆☆☆☆
TASTE :	☆☆☆☆☆
MOUTHFEEL :	☆☆☆☆☆
OVERALL RATING :	☆☆☆☆☆

ADDITIONAL NOTES

🍾 BOURBON NAME :		📅 DATE TASTED :	
🏭 DISTILLERY :		🔬 TYPE / GRADE :	
🌍 COUNTRY ORIGIN :		👥 AGE :	
🧪 SAMPLED :		🏷️ PRICE :	
🍶 BOTTLE SIZE :		🥃 ALCOHOL :	

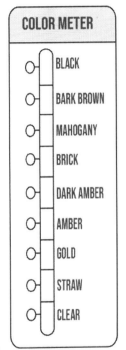

COLOR METER

- BLACK
- BARK BROWN
- MAHOGANY
- BRICK
- DARK AMBER
- AMBER
- GOLD
- STRAW
- CLEAR

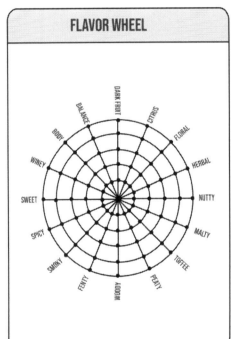

FLAVOR WHEEL

DARK FRUIT, CITRUS, FLORAL, HERBAL, NUTTY, MALTY, TOFFEE, PEATY, WOODY, FENTY, SMOKY, SPICY, SWEET, WINEY, BODY, BALANCE

FLAVOR NOTES

FINAL RATING | ADDITIONAL NOTES

🏛️ APPEARANCE :	☆☆☆☆☆	
👃 TASTE :	☆☆☆☆☆	
👄 MOUTHFEEL :	☆☆☆☆☆	
🎖️ OVERALL RATING :	☆☆☆☆☆	

🥃 BOURBON NAME :		📅 DATE TASTED :	
🏭 DISTILLERY :		🍾 TYPE / GRADE :	
🌍 COUNTRY ORIGIN :		👥 AGE :	
🧪 SAMPLED :		💲 PRICE :	
🍾 BOTTLE SIZE :		🥃 ALCOHOL :	

COLOR METER

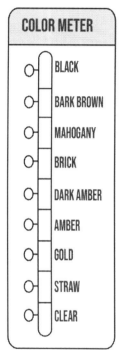

- BLACK
- BARK BROWN
- MAHOGANY
- BRICK
- DARK AMBER
- AMBER
- GOLD
- STRAW
- CLEAR

FLAVOR WHEEL

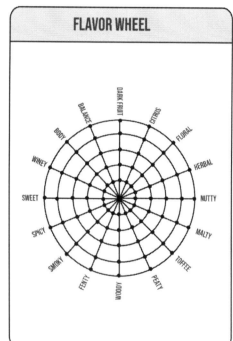

DARK FRUIT, CITRUS, FLORAL, HERBAL, NUTTY, MALTY, TOFFEE, PEATY, WOODY, FENTY, SMOKY, SPICY, SWEET, WINEY, BODY, BALANCE

FLAVOR NOTES

FINAL RATING		ADDITIONAL NOTES
🍾 APPEARANCE :	☆☆☆☆☆	
👃 TASTE :	☆☆☆☆☆	
👄 MOUTHFEEL :	☆☆☆☆☆	
🏆 OVERALL RATING :	☆☆☆☆☆	

BOURBON NAME:		**DATE TASTED:**	
DISTILLERY:		**TYPE / GRADE:**	
COUNTRY ORIGIN:		**AGE:**	
SAMPLED:		**PRICE:**	
BOTTLE SIZE:		**ALCOHOL:**	

COLOR METER

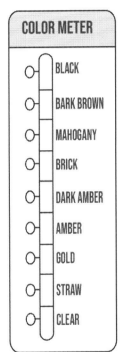

- BLACK
- BARK BROWN
- MAHOGANY
- BRICK
- DARK AMBER
- AMBER
- GOLD
- STRAW
- CLEAR

FLAVOR WHEEL

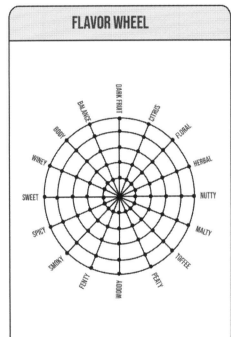

FLAVOR NOTES

FINAL RATING | ADDITIONAL NOTES

APPEARANCE:	☆☆☆☆☆	
TASTE:	☆☆☆☆☆	
MOUTHFEEL:	☆☆☆☆☆	
OVERALL RATING:	☆☆☆☆☆	

BOURBON NAME :		DATE TASTED :	
DISTILLERY :		TYPE / GRADE :	
COUNTRY ORIGIN :		AGE :	
SAMPLED :		PRICE :	
BOTTLE SIZE :		ALCOHOL :	

COLOR METER

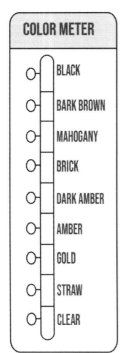

- BLACK
- BARK BROWN
- MAHOGANY
- BRICK
- DARK AMBER
- AMBER
- GOLD
- STRAW
- CLEAR

FLAVOR WHEEL

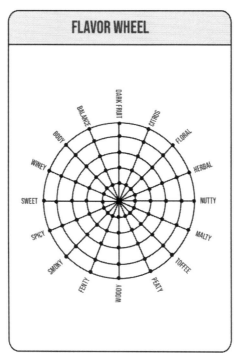

FLAVOR NOTES

FINAL RATING		ADDITIONAL NOTES
APPEARANCE :	☆☆☆☆☆	
TASTE :	☆☆☆☆☆	
MOUTHFEEL :	☆☆☆☆☆	
OVERALL RATING :	☆☆☆☆☆	

BOURBON NAME :		DATE TASTED :	
DISTILLERY :		TYPE / GRADE :	
COUNTRY ORIGIN :		AGE :	
SAMPLED :		PRICE :	
BOTTLE SIZE :		ALCOHOL :	

COLOR METER

- BLACK
- BARK BROWN
- MAHOGANY
- BRICK
- DARK AMBER
- AMBER
- GOLD
- STRAW
- CLEAR

FLAVOR WHEEL

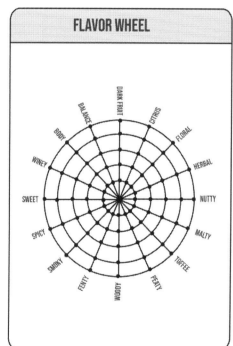

FLAVOR NOTES

FINAL RATING		ADDITIONAL NOTES
APPEARANCE :	☆☆☆☆☆	
TASTE :	☆☆☆☆☆	
MOUTHFEEL :	☆☆☆☆☆	
OVERALL RATING :	☆☆☆☆☆	

BOURBON NAME :		DATE TASTED :	
DISTILLERY :		TYPE / GRADE :	
COUNTRY ORIGIN :		AGE :	
SAMPLED :		PRICE :	
BOTTLE SIZE :		ALCOHOL :	

COLOR METER

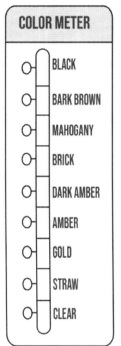

- BLACK
- BARK BROWN
- MAHOGANY
- BRICK
- DARK AMBER
- AMBER
- GOLD
- STRAW
- CLEAR

FLAVOR WHEEL

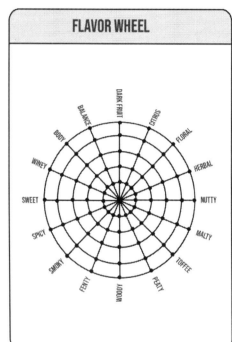

FLAVOR NOTES

FINAL RATING

		ADDITIONAL NOTES
APPEARANCE :	☆☆☆☆☆	
TASTE :	☆☆☆☆☆	
MOUTHFEEL :	☆☆☆☆☆	
OVERALL RATING :	☆☆☆☆☆	

BOURBON NAME :		**DATE TASTED :**	
DISTILLERY :		**TYPE / GRADE :**	
COUNTRY ORIGIN :		**AGE :**	
SAMPLED :		**PRICE :**	
BOTTLE SIZE :		**ALCOHOL :**	

COLOR METER

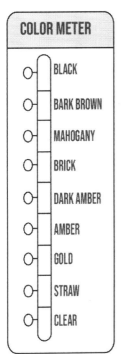

- BLACK
- BARK BROWN
- MAHOGANY
- BRICK
- DARK AMBER
- AMBER
- GOLD
- STRAW
- CLEAR

FLAVOR WHEEL

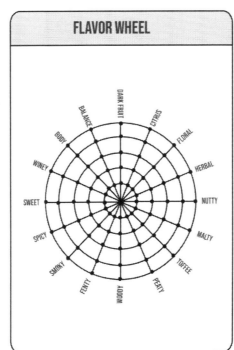

FLAVOR NOTES

FINAL RATING | ADDITIONAL NOTES

APPEARANCE :	☆☆☆☆☆	
TASTE :	☆☆☆☆☆	
MOUTHFEEL :	☆☆☆☆☆	
OVERALL RATING :	☆☆☆☆☆	

BOURBON NAME :		DATE TASTED :	
DISTILLERY :		TYPE / GRADE :	
COUNTRY ORIGIN :		AGE :	
SAMPLED :		PRICE :	
BOTTLE SIZE :		ALCOHOL :	

COLOR METER

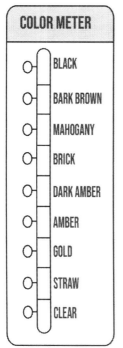

- BLACK
- BARK BROWN
- MAHOGANY
- BRICK
- DARK AMBER
- AMBER
- GOLD
- STRAW
- CLEAR

FLAVOR WHEEL

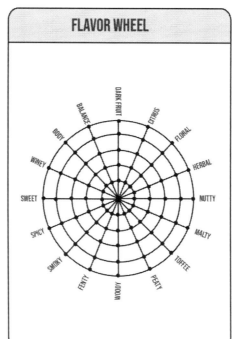

FLAVOR NOTES

FINAL RATING / ADDITIONAL NOTES

APPEARANCE :	☆☆☆☆☆	
TASTE :	☆☆☆☆☆	
MOUTHFEEL :	☆☆☆☆☆	
OVERALL RATING :	☆☆☆☆☆	

🍾 BOURBON NAME :		📅 DATE TASTED :	
🧪 DISTILLERY :		⚗️ TYPE / GRADE :	
🌍 COUNTRY ORIGIN :		👥 AGE :	
✒️ SAMPLED :		🏷️ PRICE :	
🍾 BOTTLE SIZE :		🥃 ALCOHOL :	

COLOR METER

- ○ BLACK
- ○ BARK BROWN
- ○ MAHOGANY
- ○ BRICK
- ○ DARK AMBER
- ○ AMBER
- ○ GOLD
- ○ STRAW
- ○ CLEAR

FLAVOR WHEEL

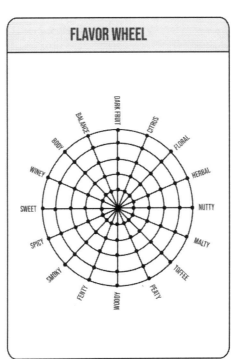

Labels: DARK FRUIT, CITRUS, FLORAL, HERBAL, NUTTY, MALTY, TOFFEE, PEATY, WOODY, FENTY, SMOKY, SPICY, SWEET, WINEY, BODY, BALANCE

FLAVOR NOTES

FINAL RATING

		ADDITIONAL NOTES
🏠 APPEARANCE :	☆☆☆☆☆	
👅 TASTE :	☆☆☆☆☆	
👄 MOUTHFEEL :	☆☆☆☆☆	
🏆 OVERALL RATING :	☆☆☆☆☆	

BOURBON NAME :		DATE TASTED :	
DISTILLERY :		TYPE / GRADE :	
COUNTRY ORIGIN :		AGE :	
SAMPLED :		PRICE :	
BOTTLE SIZE :		ALCOHOL :	

COLOR METER

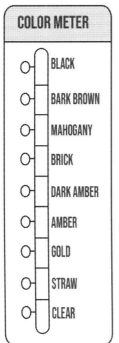

- BLACK
- BARK BROWN
- MAHOGANY
- BRICK
- DARK AMBER
- AMBER
- GOLD
- STRAW
- CLEAR

FLAVOR WHEEL

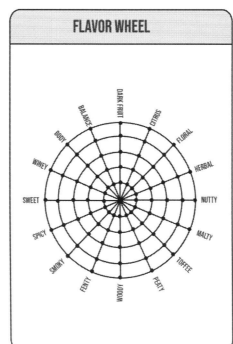

FLAVOR NOTES

FINAL RATING		ADDITIONAL NOTES
APPEARANCE :	☆☆☆☆☆	
TASTE :	☆☆☆☆☆	
MOUTHFEEL :	☆☆☆☆☆	
OVERALL RATING :	☆☆☆☆☆	

BOURBON NAME :		DATE TASTED :	
DISTILLERY :		TYPE / GRADE :	
COUNTRY ORIGIN :		AGE :	
SAMPLED :		PRICE :	
BOTTLE SIZE :		ALCOHOL :	

COLOR METER

- BLACK
- BARK BROWN
- MAHOGANY
- BRICK
- DARK AMBER
- AMBER
- GOLD
- STRAW
- CLEAR

FLAVOR WHEEL

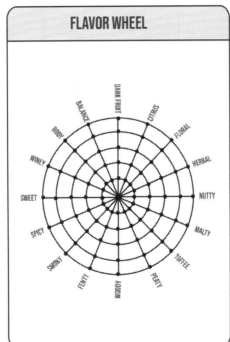

DARK FRUIT, CITRUS, FLORAL, HERBAL, NUTTY, MALTY, TOFFEE, PEATY, WOODY, FENTY, SMOKY, SPICY, SWEET, WINEY, BODY, BALANCE

FLAVOR NOTES

FINAL RATING

		ADDITIONAL NOTES
APPEARANCE :	☆☆☆☆☆	
TASTE :	☆☆☆☆☆	
MOUTHFEEL :	☆☆☆☆☆	
OVERALL RATING :	☆☆☆☆☆	

BOURBON NAME :		DATE TASTED :	
DISTILLERY :		TYPE / GRADE :	
COUNTRY ORIGIN :		AGE :	
SAMPLED :		PRICE :	
BOTTLE SIZE :		ALCOHOL :	

COLOR METER

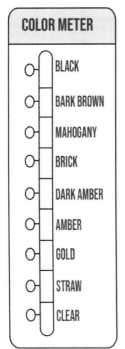

- BLACK
- BARK BROWN
- MAHOGANY
- BRICK
- DARK AMBER
- AMBER
- GOLD
- STRAW
- CLEAR

FLAVOR WHEEL

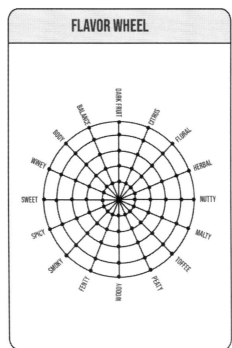

DARK FRUIT, CITRUS, FLORAL, HERBAL, NUTTY, MALTY, TOFFEE, PEATY, WOODY, FENTY, SMOKY, SPICY, SWEET, WINEY, BODY, BALANCE

FLAVOR NOTES

FINAL RATING

		ADDITIONAL NOTES
APPEARANCE :	☆☆☆☆☆	
TASTE :	☆☆☆☆☆	
MOUTHFEEL :	☆☆☆☆☆	
OVERALL RATING :	☆☆☆☆☆	

🍾 BOURBON NAME :		📅 DATE TASTED :	
🏭 DISTILLERY :		⚗️ TYPE / GRADE :	
🌍 COUNTRY ORIGIN :		👥 AGE :	
🧪 SAMPLED :		🏷️ PRICE :	
🍾 BOTTLE SIZE :		🍶 ALCOHOL :	

COLOR METER

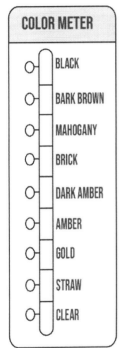

FLAVOR WHEEL

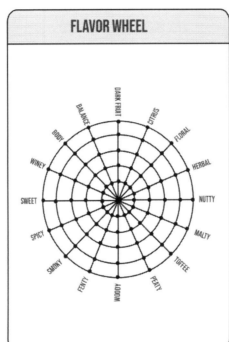

FLAVOR NOTES

FINAL RATING		ADDITIONAL NOTES
🏛️ APPEARANCE :	☆☆☆☆☆	
👅 TASTE :	☆☆☆☆☆	
👄 MOUTHFEEL :	☆☆☆☆☆	
🏆 OVERALL RATING :	☆☆☆☆☆	

BOURBON NAME :		DATE TASTED :	
DISTILLERY :		TYPE / GRADE :	
COUNTRY ORIGIN :		AGE :	
SAMPLED :		PRICE :	
BOTTLE SIZE :		ALCOHOL :	

COLOR METER

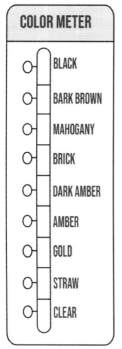

- BLACK
- BARK BROWN
- MAHOGANY
- BRICK
- DARK AMBER
- AMBER
- GOLD
- STRAW
- CLEAR

FLAVOR WHEEL

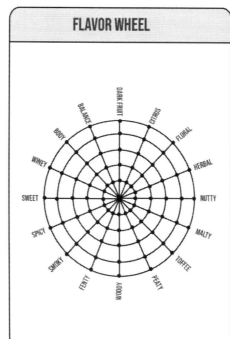

DARK FRUIT, CITRUS, FLORAL, HERBAL, NUTTY, MALTY, TOFFEE, PEATY, WOODY, FENTY, SMOKY, SPICY, SWEET, WINEY, BODY, BALANCE

FLAVOR NOTES

FINAL RATING | ADDITIONAL NOTES

APPEARANCE :	☆☆☆☆☆	
TASTE :	☆☆☆☆☆	
MOUTHFEEL :	☆☆☆☆☆	
OVERALL RATING :	☆☆☆☆☆	

🍾 BOURBON NAME :		📅 DATE TASTED :	
🏭 DISTILLERY :		🏆 TYPE / GRADE :	
🌐 COUNTRY ORIGIN :		👥 AGE :	
🥄 SAMPLED :		💰 PRICE :	
🍶 BOTTLE SIZE :		🍷 ALCOHOL :	

COLOR METER

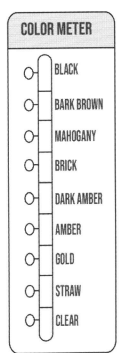

- BLACK
- BARK BROWN
- MAHOGANY
- BRICK
- DARK AMBER
- AMBER
- GOLD
- STRAW
- CLEAR

FLAVOR WHEEL

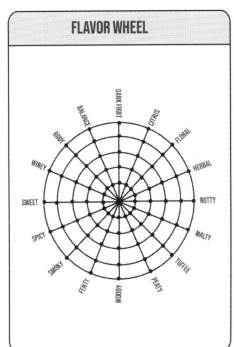

BALANCE, DARK FRUIT, CITRUS, FLORAL, BODY, HERBAL, WINEY, SWEET, NUTTY, SPICY, MALTY, SMOKY, TOFFEE, FENTY, WOODY, PEATY

FLAVOR NOTES

FINAL RATING		ADDITIONAL NOTES
🍾 APPEARANCE :	☆☆☆☆☆	
👅 TASTE :	☆☆☆☆☆	
👄 MOUTHFEEL :	☆☆☆☆☆	
🏆 OVERALL RATING :	☆☆☆☆☆	

BOURBON NAME :		DATE TASTED :	
DISTILLERY :		TYPE / GRADE :	
COUNTRY ORIGIN :		AGE :	
SAMPLED :		PRICE :	
BOTTLE SIZE :		ALCOHOL :	

COLOR METER

- BLACK
- BARK BROWN
- MAHOGANY
- BRICK
- DARK AMBER
- AMBER
- GOLD
- STRAW
- CLEAR

FLAVOR WHEEL

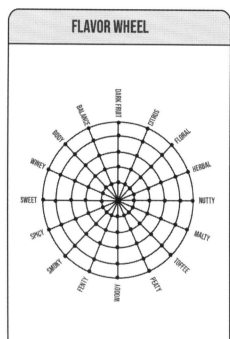

BALANCE, DARK FRUIT, CITRUS, FLORAL, BODY, HERBAL, WINEY, SWEET, NUTTY, SPICY, MALTY, SMOKY, TOFFEE, FENTY, PEATY, WOODY

FLAVOR NOTES

FINAL RATING		ADDITIONAL NOTES
APPEARANCE :	☆☆☆☆☆	
TASTE :	☆☆☆☆☆	
MOUTHFEEL :	☆☆☆☆☆	
OVERALL RATING :	☆☆☆☆☆	

🍾 BOURBON NAME :		📅 DATE TASTED :	
🏭 DISTILLERY :		⚗️ TYPE / GRADE :	
🌍 COUNTRY ORIGIN :		👥 AGE :	
🧪 SAMPLED :		💰 PRICE :	
🍾 BOTTLE SIZE :		🥃 ALCOHOL :	

COLOR METER

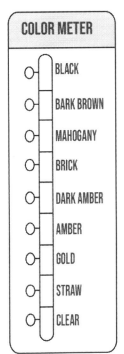

- BLACK
- BARK BROWN
- MAHOGANY
- BRICK
- DARK AMBER
- AMBER
- GOLD
- STRAW
- CLEAR

FLAVOR WHEEL

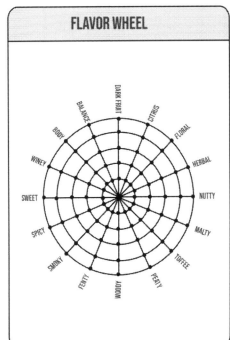

FLAVOR NOTES

FINAL RATING		ADDITIONAL NOTES
🍺 APPEARANCE :	☆☆☆☆☆	
👃 TASTE :	☆☆☆☆☆	
👄 MOUTHFEEL :	☆☆☆☆☆	
🏆 OVERALL RATING :	☆☆☆☆☆	

BOURBON NAME :		DATE TASTED :	
DISTILLERY :		TYPE / GRADE :	
COUNTRY ORIGIN :		AGE :	
SAMPLED :		PRICE :	
BOTTLE SIZE :		ALCOHOL :	

COLOR METER

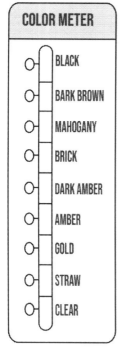

- BLACK
- BARK BROWN
- MAHOGANY
- BRICK
- DARK AMBER
- AMBER
- GOLD
- STRAW
- CLEAR

FLAVOR WHEEL

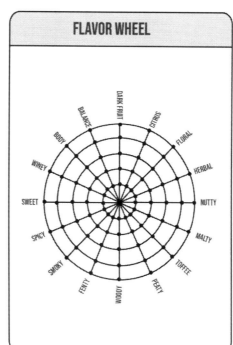

DARK FRUIT, CITRUS, FLORAL, HERBAL, NUTTY, MALTY, TOFFEE, PEATY, WOODY, FENTY, SMOKY, SPICY, SWEET, WINEY, BODY, BALANCE

FLAVOR NOTES

FINAL RATING		ADDITIONAL NOTES
APPEARANCE :	☆☆☆☆☆	
TASTE :	☆☆☆☆☆	
MOUTHFEEL :	☆☆☆☆☆	
OVERALL RATING :	☆☆☆☆☆	

BOURBON NAME :		DATE TASTED :	
DISTILLERY :		TYPE / GRADE :	
COUNTRY ORIGIN :		AGE :	
SAMPLED :		PRICE :	
BOTTLE SIZE :		ALCOHOL :	

COLOR METER

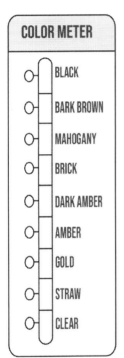

- BLACK
- BARK BROWN
- MAHOGANY
- BRICK
- DARK AMBER
- AMBER
- GOLD
- STRAW
- CLEAR

FLAVOR WHEEL

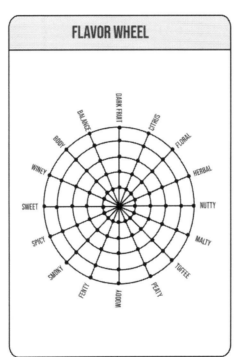

FLAVOR NOTES

FINAL RATING

		ADDITIONAL NOTES
APPEARANCE :	☆☆☆☆☆	
TASTE :	☆☆☆☆☆	
MOUTHFEEL :	☆☆☆☆☆	
OVERALL RATING :	☆☆☆☆☆	

🥃 BOURBON NAME :		📅 DATE TASTED :	
🧪 DISTILLERY :		🔬 TYPE / GRADE :	
🌐 COUNTRY ORIGIN :		👥 AGE :	
🧪 SAMPLED :		💰 PRICE :	
🍾 BOTTLE SIZE :		🥃 ALCOHOL :	

COLOR METER

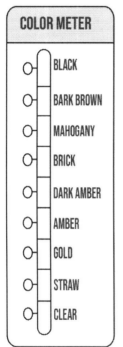

- BLACK
- BARK BROWN
- MAHOGANY
- BRICK
- DARK AMBER
- AMBER
- GOLD
- STRAW
- CLEAR

FLAVOR WHEEL

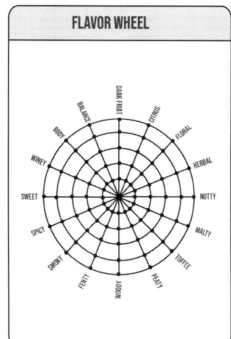

FLAVOR NOTES

FINAL RATING		ADDITIONAL NOTES
🍾 APPEARANCE :	☆☆☆☆☆	
👃 TASTE :	☆☆☆☆☆	
👄 MOUTHFEEL :	☆☆☆☆☆	
🏆 OVERALL RATING :	☆☆☆☆☆	

🥃 BOURBON NAME :		📅 DATE TASTED :	
🏭 DISTILLERY :		🥃 TYPE / GRADE :	
🌍 COUNTRY ORIGIN :		👥 AGE :	
🖊 SAMPLED :		💰 PRICE :	
🍾 BOTTLE SIZE :		🍶 ALCOHOL :	

COLOR METER

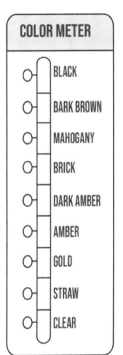

- BLACK
- BARK BROWN
- MAHOGANY
- BRICK
- DARK AMBER
- AMBER
- GOLD
- STRAW
- CLEAR

FLAVOR WHEEL

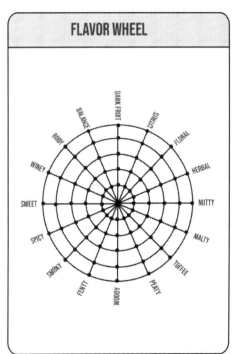

DARK FRUIT, CITRUS, FLORAL, HERBAL, NUTTY, MALTY, TOFFEE, PEATY, WOODY, FENTY, SMOKY, SPICY, SWEET, WINEY, BODY, BALANCE

FLAVOR NOTES

FINAL RATING		ADDITIONAL NOTES
🍺 APPEARANCE :	☆☆☆☆☆	
👅 TASTE :	☆☆☆☆☆	
👄 MOUTHFEEL :	☆☆☆☆☆	
🥃 OVERALL RATING :	☆☆☆☆☆	

BOURBON NAME :		DATE TASTED :	
DISTILLERY :		TYPE / GRADE :	
COUNTRY ORIGIN :		AGE :	
SAMPLED :		PRICE :	
BOTTLE SIZE :		ALCOHOL :	

COLOR METER

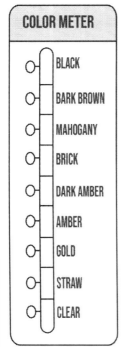

- BLACK
- BARK BROWN
- MAHOGANY
- BRICK
- DARK AMBER
- AMBER
- GOLD
- STRAW
- CLEAR

FLAVOR WHEEL

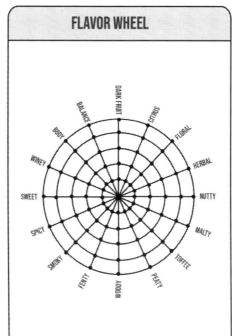

FLAVOR NOTES

FINAL RATING		ADDITIONAL NOTES
APPEARANCE :	☆☆☆☆☆	
TASTE :	☆☆☆☆☆	
MOUTHFEEL :	☆☆☆☆☆	
OVERALL RATING :	☆☆☆☆☆	

BOURBON NAME :		DATE TASTED :	
DISTILLERY :		TYPE / GRADE :	
COUNTRY ORIGIN :		AGE :	
SAMPLED :		PRICE :	
BOTTLE SIZE :		ALCOHOL :	

COLOR METER

- BLACK
- BARK BROWN
- MAHOGANY
- BRICK
- DARK AMBER
- AMBER
- GOLD
- STRAW
- CLEAR

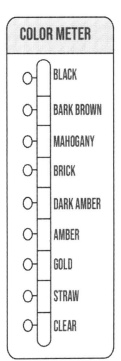

FLAVOR WHEEL

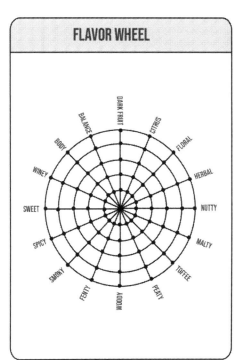

FLAVOR NOTES

FINAL RATING

		ADDITIONAL NOTES
APPEARANCE :	☆☆☆☆☆	
TASTE :	☆☆☆☆☆	
MOUTHFEEL :	☆☆☆☆☆	
OVERALL RATING :	☆☆☆☆☆	

BOURBON NAME :		DATE TASTED :	
DISTILLERY :		TYPE / GRADE :	
COUNTRY ORIGIN :		AGE :	
SAMPLED :		PRICE :	
BOTTLE SIZE :		ALCOHOL :	

COLOR METER

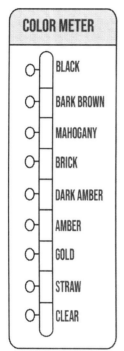

- BLACK
- BARK BROWN
- MAHOGANY
- BRICK
- DARK AMBER
- AMBER
- GOLD
- STRAW
- CLEAR

FLAVOR WHEEL

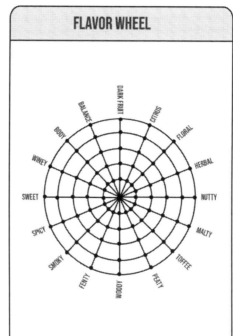

FLAVOR NOTES

FINAL RATING | ADDITIONAL NOTES

APPEARANCE :	☆☆☆☆☆	
TASTE :	☆☆☆☆☆	
MOUTHFEEL :	☆☆☆☆☆	
OVERALL RATING :	☆☆☆☆☆	

BOURBON NAME :		DATE TASTED :	
DISTILLERY :		TYPE / GRADE :	
COUNTRY ORIGIN :		AGE :	
SAMPLED :		PRICE :	
BOTTLE SIZE :		ALCOHOL :	

COLOR METER

- BLACK
- BARK BROWN
- MAHOGANY
- BRICK
- DARK AMBER
- AMBER
- GOLD
- STRAW
- CLEAR

FLAVOR WHEEL

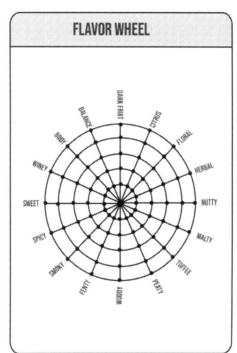

FLAVOR NOTES

FINAL RATING		ADDITIONAL NOTES
APPEARANCE :	☆☆☆☆☆	
TASTE :	☆☆☆☆☆	
MOUTHFEEL :	☆☆☆☆☆	
OVERALL RATING :	☆☆☆☆☆	

BOURBON NAME :		DATE TASTED :	
DISTILLERY :		TYPE / GRADE :	
COUNTRY ORIGIN :		AGE :	
SAMPLED :		PRICE :	
BOTTLE SIZE :		ALCOHOL :	

COLOR METER

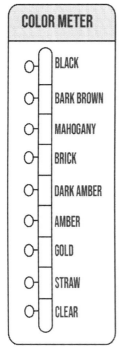

- BLACK
- BARK BROWN
- MAHOGANY
- BRICK
- DARK AMBER
- AMBER
- GOLD
- STRAW
- CLEAR

FLAVOR WHEEL

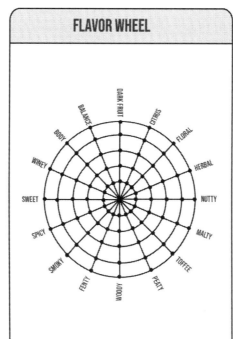

DARK FRUIT, CITRUS, FLORAL, HERBAL, NUTTY, MALTY, TOFFEE, PEATY, WOODY, FRUITY, SMOKY, SPICY, SWEET, WINEY, BODY, BALANCE

FLAVOR NOTES

FINAL RATING

APPEARANCE :	☆☆☆☆☆
TASTE :	☆☆☆☆☆
MOUTHFEEL :	☆☆☆☆☆
OVERALL RATING :	☆☆☆☆☆

ADDITIONAL NOTES

BOURBON NAME :		**DATE TASTED :**	
DISTILLERY :		**TYPE / GRADE :**	
COUNTRY ORIGIN :		**AGE :**	
SAMPLED :		**PRICE :**	
BOTTLE SIZE :		**ALCOHOL :**	

COLOR METER

- BLACK
- BARK BROWN
- MAHOGANY
- BRICK
- DARK AMBER
- AMBER
- GOLD
- STRAW
- CLEAR

FLAVOR WHEEL

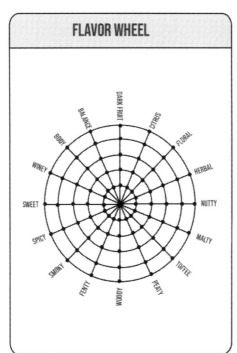

FLAVOR NOTES

FINAL RATING

APPEARANCE :	☆☆☆☆☆
TASTE :	☆☆☆☆☆
MOUTHFEEL :	☆☆☆☆☆
OVERALL RATING :	☆☆☆☆☆

ADDITIONAL NOTES

BOURBON NAME :		DATE TASTED :	
DISTILLERY :		TYPE / GRADE :	
COUNTRY ORIGIN :		AGE :	
SAMPLED :		PRICE :	
BOTTLE SIZE :		ALCOHOL :	

COLOR METER

- BLACK
- BARK BROWN
- MAHOGANY
- BRICK
- DARK AMBER
- AMBER
- GOLD
- STRAW
- CLEAR

FLAVOR WHEEL

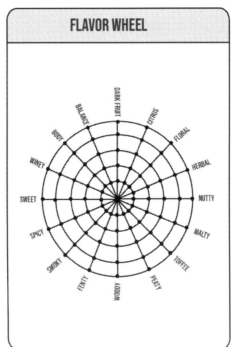

DARK FRUIT, CITRUS, FLORAL, HERBAL, NUTTY, MALTY, TOFFEE, PEATY, WOODY, FRUITY, SMOKY, SPICY, SWEET, WINEY, BODY, BALANCE

FLAVOR NOTES

FINAL RATING | ADDITIONAL NOTES

APPEARANCE :	☆☆☆☆☆	
TASTE :	☆☆☆☆☆	
MOUTHFEEL :	☆☆☆☆☆	
OVERALL RATING :	☆☆☆☆☆	

BOURBON NAME :		DATE TASTED :	
DISTILLERY :		TYPE / GRADE :	
COUNTRY ORIGIN :		AGE :	
SAMPLED :		PRICE :	
BOTTLE SIZE :		ALCOHOL :	

COLOR METER

- BLACK
- BARK BROWN
- MAHOGANY
- BRICK
- DARK AMBER
- AMBER
- GOLD
- STRAW
- CLEAR

FLAVOR WHEEL

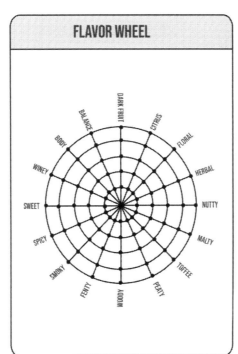

FLAVOR NOTES

FINAL RATING		ADDITIONAL NOTES
APPEARANCE :	☆☆☆☆☆	
TASTE :	☆☆☆☆☆	
MOUTHFEEL :	☆☆☆☆☆	
OVERALL RATING :	☆☆☆☆☆	

BOURBON NAME :		DATE TASTED :	
DISTILLERY :		TYPE / GRADE :	
COUNTRY ORIGIN :		AGE :	
SAMPLED :		PRICE :	
BOTTLE SIZE :		ALCOHOL :	

COLOR METER

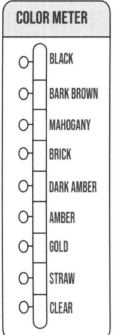

- BLACK
- BARK BROWN
- MAHOGANY
- BRICK
- DARK AMBER
- AMBER
- GOLD
- STRAW
- CLEAR

FLAVOR WHEEL

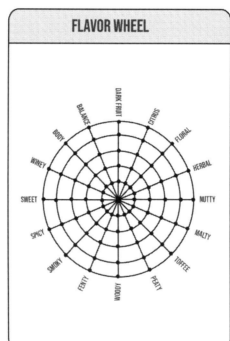

DARK FRUIT, CITRUS, FLORAL, HERBAL, NUTTY, MALTY, TOFFEE, PEATY, WOODY, FRUITY, SMOKY, SPICY, SWEET, WINEY, BODY, BALANCE

FLAVOR NOTES

FINAL RATING | ADDITIONAL NOTES

APPEARANCE :	☆☆☆☆☆	
TASTE :	☆☆☆☆☆	
MOUTHFEEL :	☆☆☆☆☆	
OVERALL RATING :	☆☆☆☆☆	

BOURBON NAME :		DATE TASTED :	
DISTILLERY :		TYPE / GRADE :	
COUNTRY ORIGIN :		AGE :	
SAMPLED :		PRICE :	
BOTTLE SIZE :		ALCOHOL :	

COLOR METER

- BLACK
- BARK BROWN
- MAHOGANY
- BRICK
- DARK AMBER
- AMBER
- GOLD
- STRAW
- CLEAR

FLAVOR WHEEL

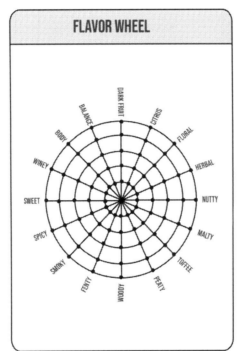

DARK FRUIT, CITRUS, FLORAL, HERBAL, NUTTY, MALTY, TOFFEE, PEATY, AROMA, FENTY, SMOKY, SPICY, SWEET, WINEY, BODY, BALANCE

FLAVOR NOTES

FINAL RATING

APPEARANCE :	☆☆☆☆☆
TASTE :	☆☆☆☆☆
MOUTHFEEL :	☆☆☆☆☆
OVERALL RATING :	☆☆☆☆☆

ADDITIONAL NOTES

BOURBON NAME :		DATE TASTED :	
DISTILLERY :		TYPE / GRADE :	
COUNTRY ORIGIN :		AGE :	
SAMPLED :		PRICE :	
BOTTLE SIZE :		ALCOHOL :	

COLOR METER

- BLACK
- BARK BROWN
- MAHOGANY
- BRICK
- DARK AMBER
- AMBER
- GOLD
- STRAW
- CLEAR

FLAVOR WHEEL

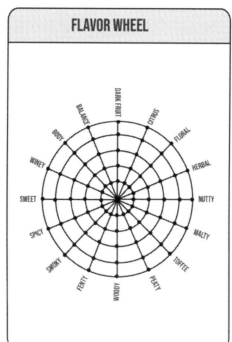

DARK FRUIT, CITRUS, FLORAL, HERBAL, NUTTY, MALTY, TOFFEE, PEATY, WOODY, FRUITY, SMOKY, SPICY, SWEET, WINEY, BODY, BALANCE

FLAVOR NOTES

FINAL RATING | ADDITIONAL NOTES

APPEARANCE :	☆☆☆☆☆	
TASTE :	☆☆☆☆☆	
MOUTHFEEL :	☆☆☆☆☆	
OVERALL RATING :	☆☆☆☆☆	

BOURBON NAME :		DATE TASTED :	
DISTILLERY :		TYPE / GRADE :	
COUNTRY ORIGIN :		AGE :	
SAMPLED :		PRICE :	
BOTTLE SIZE :		ALCOHOL :	

COLOR METER

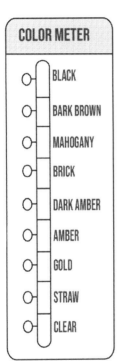

- BLACK
- BARK BROWN
- MAHOGANY
- BRICK
- DARK AMBER
- AMBER
- GOLD
- STRAW
- CLEAR

FLAVOR WHEEL

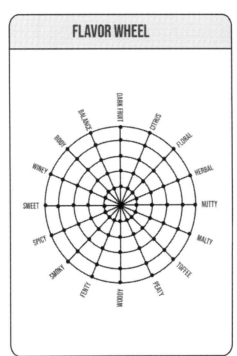

FLAVOR NOTES

FINAL RATING

		ADDITIONAL NOTES
APPEARANCE :	☆☆☆☆☆	
TASTE :	☆☆☆☆☆	
MOUTHFEEL :	☆☆☆☆☆	
OVERALL RATING :	☆☆☆☆☆	

BOURBON NAME :		DATE TASTED :	
DISTILLERY :		TYPE / GRADE :	
COUNTRY ORIGIN :		AGE :	
SAMPLED :		PRICE :	
BOTTLE SIZE :		ALCOHOL :	

COLOR METER

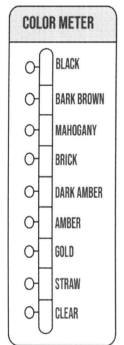

- BLACK
- BARK BROWN
- MAHOGANY
- BRICK
- DARK AMBER
- AMBER
- GOLD
- STRAW
- CLEAR

FLAVOR WHEEL

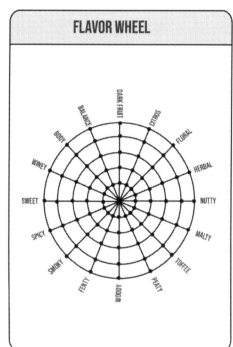

FLAVOR NOTES

FINAL RATING		ADDITIONAL NOTES
APPEARANCE :	☆☆☆☆☆	
TASTE :	☆☆☆☆☆	
MOUTHFEEL :	☆☆☆☆☆	
OVERALL RATING :	☆☆☆☆☆	

BOURBON NAME :		DATE TASTED :	
DISTILLERY :		TYPE / GRADE :	
COUNTRY ORIGIN :		AGE :	
SAMPLED :		PRICE :	
BOTTLE SIZE :		ALCOHOL :	

COLOR METER

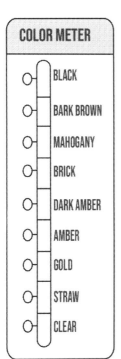

- BLACK
- BARK BROWN
- MAHOGANY
- BRICK
- DARK AMBER
- AMBER
- GOLD
- STRAW
- CLEAR

FLAVOR WHEEL

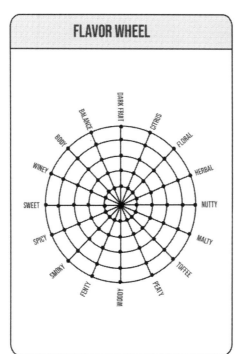

FLAVOR NOTES

FINAL RATING		ADDITIONAL NOTES
APPEARANCE :	☆☆☆☆☆	
TASTE :	☆☆☆☆☆	
MOUTHFEEL :	☆☆☆☆☆	
OVERALL RATING :	☆☆☆☆☆	

🥃 BOURBON NAME :		📅 DATE TASTED :	
⚗️ DISTILLERY :		🧪 TYPE / GRADE :	
🌍 COUNTRY ORIGIN :		👥 AGE :	
🔬 SAMPLED :		💰 PRICE :	
🍾 BOTTLE SIZE :		🥃 ALCOHOL :	

COLOR METER

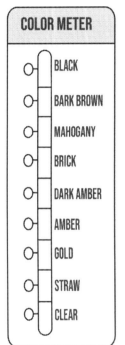

FLAVOR WHEEL

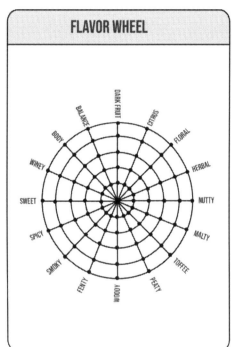

FLAVOR NOTES

FINAL RATING		ADDITIONAL NOTES
🏛️ APPEARANCE :	☆☆☆☆☆	
👃 TASTE :	☆☆☆☆☆	
👄 MOUTHFEEL :	☆☆☆☆☆	
🏆 OVERALL RATING :	☆☆☆☆☆	

BOURBON NAME :		DATE TASTED :	
DISTILLERY :		TYPE / GRADE :	
COUNTRY ORIGIN :		AGE :	
SAMPLED :		PRICE :	
BOTTLE SIZE :		ALCOHOL :	

COLOR METER

○ BLACK
○ BARK BROWN
○ MAHOGANY
○ BRICK
○ DARK AMBER
○ AMBER
○ GOLD
○ STRAW
○ CLEAR

FLAVOR WHEEL

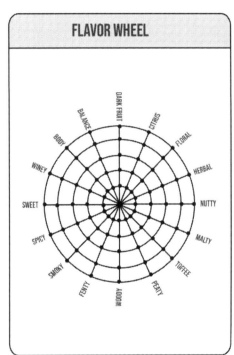

FLAVOR NOTES

FINAL RATING		ADDITIONAL NOTES
APPEARANCE :	☆☆☆☆☆	
TASTE :	☆☆☆☆☆	
MOUTHFEEL :	☆☆☆☆☆	
OVERALL RATING :	☆☆☆☆☆	

BOURBON NAME :		DATE TASTED :	
DISTILLERY :		TYPE / GRADE :	
COUNTRY ORIGIN :		AGE :	
SAMPLED :		PRICE :	
BOTTLE SIZE :		ALCOHOL :	

COLOR METER

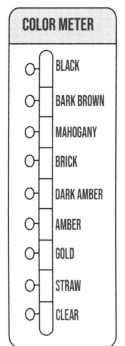

- BLACK
- BARK BROWN
- MAHOGANY
- BRICK
- DARK AMBER
- AMBER
- GOLD
- STRAW
- CLEAR

FLAVOR WHEEL

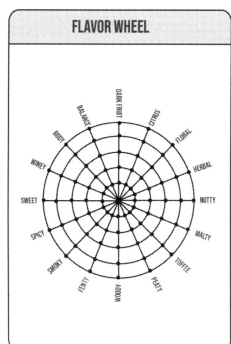

FLAVOR NOTES

FINAL RATING		ADDITIONAL NOTES
APPEARANCE :	☆☆☆☆☆	
TASTE :	☆☆☆☆☆	
MOUTHFEEL :	☆☆☆☆☆	
OVERALL RATING :	☆☆☆☆☆	

BOURBON NAME :		DATE TASTED :	
DISTILLERY :		TYPE / GRADE :	
COUNTRY ORIGIN :		AGE :	
SAMPLED :		PRICE :	
BOTTLE SIZE :		ALCOHOL :	

COLOR METER

- BLACK
- BARK BROWN
- MAHOGANY
- BRICK
- DARK AMBER
- AMBER
- GOLD
- STRAW
- CLEAR

FLAVOR WHEEL

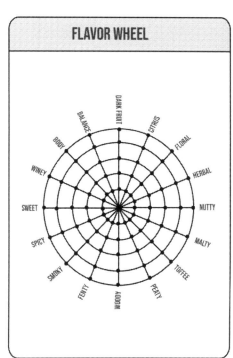

DARK FRUIT, CITRUS, FLORAL, HERBAL, NUTTY, MALTY, TOFFEE, PEATY, AGOOM, FENTY, SMOKY, SPICY, SWEET, WINEY, BODY, BALANCE

FLAVOR NOTES

FINAL RATING		ADDITIONAL NOTES
APPEARANCE :	☆☆☆☆☆	
TASTE :	☆☆☆☆☆	
MOUTHFEEL :	☆☆☆☆☆	
OVERALL RATING :	☆☆☆☆☆	

BOURBON NAME :		DATE TASTED :	
DISTILLERY :		TYPE / GRADE :	
COUNTRY ORIGIN :		AGE :	
SAMPLED :		PRICE :	
BOTTLE SIZE :		ALCOHOL :	

COLOR METER

- BLACK
- BARK BROWN
- MAHOGANY
- BRICK
- DARK AMBER
- AMBER
- GOLD
- STRAW
- CLEAR

FLAVOR WHEEL

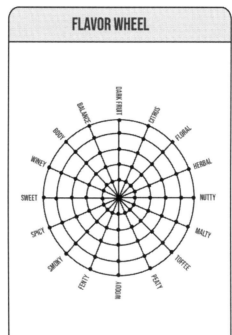

DARK FRUIT, CITRUS, FLORAL, HERBAL, NUTTY, MALTY, TOFFEE, PEATY, WOODY, PEATY, SMOKY, SPICY, SWEET, WINEY, BODY, BALANCE

FLAVOR NOTES

FINAL RATING | ADDITIONAL NOTES

APPEARANCE :	☆☆☆☆☆	
TASTE :	☆☆☆☆☆	
MOUTHFEEL :	☆☆☆☆☆	
OVERALL RATING :	☆☆☆☆☆	

BOURBON NAME :		DATE TASTED :	
DISTILLERY :		TYPE / GRADE :	
COUNTRY ORIGIN :		AGE :	
SAMPLED :		PRICE :	
BOTTLE SIZE :		ALCOHOL :	

COLOR METER

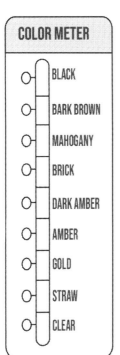

- BLACK
- BARK BROWN
- MAHOGANY
- BRICK
- DARK AMBER
- AMBER
- GOLD
- STRAW
- CLEAR

FLAVOR WHEEL

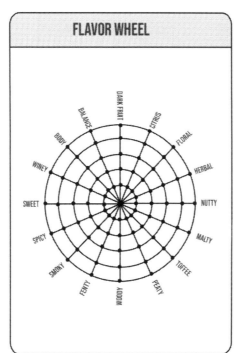

FLAVOR NOTES

FINAL RATING | ADDITIONAL NOTES

APPEARANCE :	☆☆☆☆☆	
TASTE :	☆☆☆☆☆	
MOUTHFEEL :	☆☆☆☆☆	
OVERALL RATING :	☆☆☆☆☆	

BOURBON NAME:		**DATE TASTED:**	
DISTILLERY:		**TYPE / GRADE:**	
COUNTRY ORIGIN:		**AGE:**	
SAMPLED:		**PRICE:**	
BOTTLE SIZE:		**ALCOHOL:**	

COLOR METER

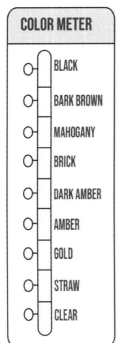

- BLACK
- BARK BROWN
- MAHOGANY
- BRICK
- DARK AMBER
- AMBER
- GOLD
- STRAW
- CLEAR

FLAVOR WHEEL

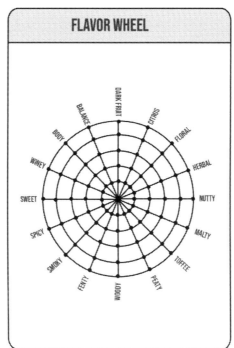

FLAVOR NOTES

FINAL RATING

		ADDITIONAL NOTES
APPEARANCE:	☆☆☆☆☆	
TASTE:	☆☆☆☆☆	
MOUTHFEEL:	☆☆☆☆☆	
OVERALL RATING:	☆☆☆☆☆	

BOURBON NAME :		DATE TASTED :	
DISTILLERY :		TYPE / GRADE :	
COUNTRY ORIGIN :		AGE :	
SAMPLED :		PRICE :	
BOTTLE SIZE :		ALCOHOL :	

COLOR METER

- BLACK
- BARK BROWN
- MAHOGANY
- BRICK
- DARK AMBER
- AMBER
- GOLD
- STRAW
- CLEAR

FLAVOR WHEEL

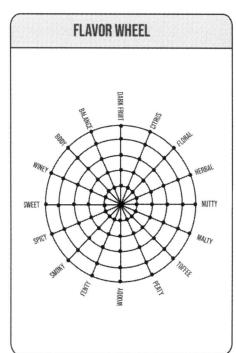

FLAVOR NOTES

FINAL RATING | ADDITIONAL NOTES

APPEARANCE :	☆☆☆☆☆	
TASTE :	☆☆☆☆☆	
MOUTHFEEL :	☆☆☆☆☆	
OVERALL RATING :	☆☆☆☆☆	

BOURBON NAME :		DATE TASTED :	
DISTILLERY :		TYPE / GRADE :	
COUNTRY ORIGIN :		AGE :	
SAMPLED :		PRICE :	
BOTTLE SIZE :		ALCOHOL :	

COLOR METER

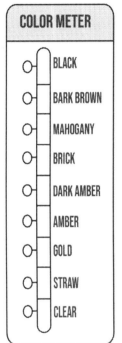

- BLACK
- BARK BROWN
- MAHOGANY
- BRICK
- DARK AMBER
- AMBER
- GOLD
- STRAW
- CLEAR

FLAVOR WHEEL

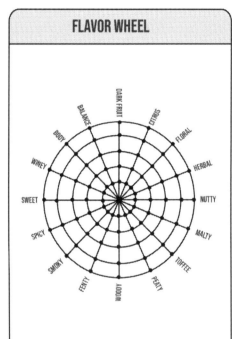

FLAVOR NOTES

FINAL RATING | ADDITIONAL NOTES

APPEARANCE :	☆☆☆☆☆	
TASTE :	☆☆☆☆☆	
MOUTHFEEL :	☆☆☆☆☆	
OVERALL RATING :	☆☆☆☆☆	

BOURBON NAME :		DATE TASTED :	
DISTILLERY :		TYPE / GRADE :	
COUNTRY ORIGIN :		AGE :	
SAMPLED :		PRICE :	
BOTTLE SIZE :		ALCOHOL :	

COLOR METER

- BLACK
- BARK BROWN
- MAHOGANY
- BRICK
- DARK AMBER
- AMBER
- GOLD
- STRAW
- CLEAR

FLAVOR WHEEL

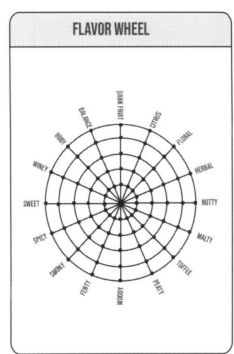

DARK FRUIT, CITRUS, FLORAL, HERBAL, NUTTY, MALTY, TOFFEE, PEATY, WOODY, FENTY, SMOKY, SPICY, SWEET, WINEY, BODY, BALANCE

FLAVOR NOTES

FINAL RATING		ADDITIONAL NOTES
APPEARANCE :	☆☆☆☆☆	
TASTE :	☆☆☆☆☆	
MOUTHFEEL :	☆☆☆☆☆	
OVERALL RATING :	☆☆☆☆☆	

BOURBON NAME :		DATE TASTED :	
DISTILLERY :		TYPE / GRADE :	
COUNTRY ORIGIN :		AGE :	
SAMPLED :		PRICE :	
BOTTLE SIZE :		ALCOHOL :	

COLOR METER

- BLACK
- BARK BROWN
- MAHOGANY
- BRICK
- DARK AMBER
- AMBER
- GOLD
- STRAW
- CLEAR

FLAVOR WHEEL

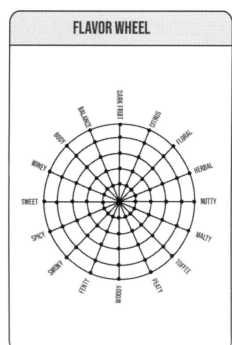

DARK FRUIT, CITRUS, FLORAL, HERBAL, NUTTY, MALTY, TOFFEE, PEATY, WOODY, PEATY, SMOKY, SPICY, SWEET, WINEY, BODY, BALANCE

FLAVOR NOTES

FINAL RATING | ADDITIONAL NOTES

APPEARANCE :	☆☆☆☆☆	
TASTE :	☆☆☆☆☆	
MOUTHFEEL :	☆☆☆☆☆	
OVERALL RATING :	☆☆☆☆☆	

BOURBON NAME :		DATE TASTED :	
DISTILLERY :		TYPE / GRADE :	
COUNTRY ORIGIN :		AGE :	
SAMPLED :		PRICE :	
BOTTLE SIZE :		ALCOHOL :	

COLOR METER

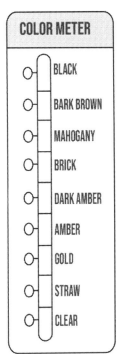

- BLACK
- BARK BROWN
- MAHOGANY
- BRICK
- DARK AMBER
- AMBER
- GOLD
- STRAW
- CLEAR

FLAVOR WHEEL

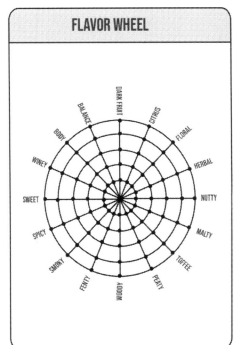

DARK FRUIT, CITRUS, FLORAL, HERBAL, NUTTY, MALTY, TOFFEE, PEATY, AROOM, FENTY, SMOKY, SPICY, SWEET, WINEY, BODY, BALANCE

FLAVOR NOTES

FINAL RATING		ADDITIONAL NOTES
APPEARANCE :	☆☆☆☆☆	
TASTE :	☆☆☆☆☆	
MOUTHFEEL :	☆☆☆☆☆	
OVERALL RATING :	☆☆☆☆☆	

🍾 BOURBON NAME :		📅 DATE TASTED :	
🏭 DISTILLERY :		🧪 TYPE / GRADE :	
🌐 COUNTRY ORIGIN :		👥 AGE :	
🧪 SAMPLED :		💰 PRICE :	
🍾 BOTTLE SIZE :		🥃 ALCOHOL :	

COLOR METER

- BLACK
- BARK BROWN
- MAHOGANY
- BRICK
- DARK AMBER
- AMBER
- GOLD
- STRAW
- CLEAR

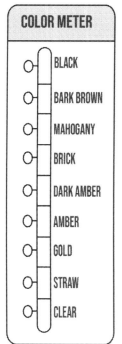

FLAVOR WHEEL

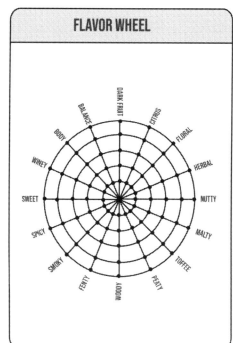

FLAVOR NOTES

FINAL RATING		ADDITIONAL NOTES
🏆 APPEARANCE :	☆☆☆☆☆	
👃 TASTE :	☆☆☆☆☆	
👄 MOUTHFEEL :	☆☆☆☆☆	
🏅 OVERALL RATING :	☆☆☆☆☆	